Ecumenism and the Future
of the Church

———————————— YVES CONGAR, O.P.

Ecumenism and the Future
of the Church

THE PRIORY PRESS, CHICAGO, ILL.

The first six chapters of this book are a translation of *Aspects de l'Oecuménisme*, by Yves Congar, O.P., originally published in French by La Pensée Catholique, Bruxelles. Translations have been made into Italian, Castilian, and Catalan. English translation by John C. Guinness. Chapter Seven is a translation of "L'Avenir de l'Eglise," by the same author, originally published in French by Librairie Arthème Fayard, Paris, in *L'Avenir* (Semaine du C.C.I.F., 1963). English translation by Geraldine F. McIntosh.

Revisores Ordinis: Thomas C. Donlan, O.P.; Bernard O'Riley, O.P. *Imprimi potest*: Gilbert J. Graham, O.P., Provincial. *Nihil obstat*: Thomas C. Donlan, O.P., Bernard O'Riley, O.P., Censores Deputati. *Imprimatur*: Most Rev. Cletus F. O'Donnell, J.C.D., Vicar General, Archdiocese of Chicago, November 7, 1966.

Library of Congress Catalogue Number 67-14012
Entire English translation copyright © 1967 by
THE PRIORY PRESS
1165 East 54 Place, Chicago, Illinois 60615
Manufactured in the United States of America

Preface

It is always a profound experience to read a book of Father Yves Congar. Protestants have known him through his books as a creative and provocative scholar whose research and studies have paved the way for a fresh understanding and appreciation of Christian faith and of Roman Catholicism. He is received in Protestant circles as one of the handful of Roman Catholic ecumenical heralds who first sounded the call for a new spirit of mutual respect, understanding, and love between Christians from differing traditions. His theological scholarship provided one of the most provocative bases for a rapprochement between Catholics and Protestants.

This small volume is a collection of essays delivered at various times and places as lectures. Most appear to be written before Vatican II, though the last, "The Future of the Church," is post-Vatican II. Three things stand out in this little book. The spirit of the author is clearly reflected in all essays. Congar's hopes for the future of the Church shine through each lecture, and his awareness of the long preparation and the complex background of the present ecumenical epoch runs through the volume.

One cannot judge which of these three emphases is primary in the book. All three are present to some degree in each essay, and together they mark the special contribution of the book. The spiritual depth so evident to all who know Father Congar shines through virtually every page. Prayer is not a technique for him to be employed in an effort to achieve mutual understanding and the unity of the Church. It is the bedrock of the Christian life which makes possible the search together for the unity which is already present in the Christ. Without the profound resources of a deep spirituality the search for ecumenicity will be purely external and institutional.

The remarkable openness of Father Congar is demonstrated again in these pages. He has no pat answers or simple solutions to ecumenical problems or possibilities. He opens himself to the truth embodied in Orthodoxy and in Protestantism. Because he genuinely seeks to understand and to learn from them he can teach them. Perhaps this openness is most evident in his constant references to the reality and the role of the Holy Spirit in the search for oneness. He is prepared for new leadings of the Spirit beyond our present projections and even our imagination as the Church moves ahead in the ecumenical age. Yet his openness is not to be mistaken for vagueness or uncertainty. Father Congar stands firmly in the midst of the Roman Catholic Church, but because he knows where he stands, he does not have to be narrow or unyielding. Believing deeply in the efficacy and presence of the

Holy Spirit, he can seriously expect and be open to the mysterious work of the Spirit.

One of the salutary features of the book is Father Congar's acute awareness of the various historical stages through which the Church has come to her present ecumenical moment. The first chapter is a succinct and masterful summary of these various stages. It is a necessary reminder that the present did not drop from the heavens; it is the consequence of a long, painful, but very creative development. Since the East-West schism and the Reformation, the various branches of Christianity have had differing forms of contact, particularly in the West. It is absolutely necessary to understand what transpired over these centuries if one wishes to see where the Church is today. There is no substitute—personal piety or theological sophistication —for the maturation process of history which leads to a fullness of time, a peculiar moment in history towards which all tends, for which all work and pray, but which only God can bring to fulfillment.

Congar's references, in almost all chapters, to these various historical developments is both a resource and a warning to all engaged in the ecumenical task. It is a resource that many overlook as they enthusiastically plunge into the ecumenical endeavor. It is a resource that is overlooked with great danger. Various forms of dialogue and efforts at reunion have been tried in the past. Some have been bypassed completely in history; others have become the base on which all build today. Yet today, in its own way, has its own uniqueness, its moment of fulfillment. It is a combination of an awareness of the past attempts and their relation to present efforts, plus an astute analysis of the dynamics of today's endeavors that marks Congar's essays.

In the concluding essay, written after Vatican II, Father Congar sketches out his hopes for the future of the Church. These hopes are shared by millions of sensitive Christians. He calls for the Church to be less of the world and more to the world, a view which is identical with that now in the foreground of Protestantism. Though it appears that Protestantism needs more institutionalism over against an excessive individualism and Catholicism requires more individual participation and responsibility over against an excessive institutionalism, the fact is that both require a new form of institutional life in the modern world and a new kind of individual participation. It is not a question primarily of redressing a balance, it is a question of the nature and quality of the historic expressions of the Christian community. Father Congar has marked this so well in his statement that Christianity has moved from a vast Church in a small, stable Western World to a small Church in a vast and rapidly changing world. Again the terms small and vast are not quantitative; though they are also that, they are primarily qualitative.

Father Congar dares to dream dreams as do all true ecumenically minded sons of the Churches, and these dreams are not foolishness. They are grounded in faith and in experience. Who could have predicted five to ten years ago where the Church would be today. The Church is in the midst of a renewal internally in order that she might give herself in service to the world, to all of mankind. It is this double movement in the life of the Church that not only permits dreams, it creates visions. Father Congar has helped us to see the possibility of a renewed Church in closer unity through fuller service not for herself but for her Lord to the world.

Jerald C. Brauer, Dean
The Divinity School
The University of Chicago
Octave of Christian Unity, 1967

Table of Contents

11

*Ecumenism and the Future
of the Church*

1

Stages of the Ecumenical Dialogue

We are often asked whether anything new is happening in the ecumenical movement, that is to say, in the world-wide efforts being made today to bring Christians together again in unity. Beyond doubt there is something new—something already under way and holding great promise for the future—and it must be told, because the world, scandalized by unsuccessful attempts at Christian unity, needs to hear it. The story of this something "new" will be related in these pages in the form of a broad and general survey of the history of Christian relations, or the confrontations between separated Christians down through the centuries. This will finally bring us to the present-day situation, characterized by the fitting name of ecumenism, to which the greater part of this study will be devoted.

An understanding of the disunity of Christians in the light of history and of differences in thought and outlook is necessary. Disunity split the East-West axis of Christendom; or rather, in Christian terms, shattered the communion between the Orient and the Occident. The rapprochement of these two expressions already

constitutes a matter for thought. Would the East and
the West be what they are at the moment on the political level, their conflict influencing the whole world,
if there had been no religious rupture between Orient
and Occident? This rupture was begun, then healed,
and begun again during the course of several centuries,
becoming final in the middle of the eleventh century.
Next, the sixteenth-century Reformation broke the vertical axis of Christendom. The North and the South
split, separating the Mediterranean peoples from the
Germanic and Nordic nations. As a consequence, some
950 million Christians, in a world of two and one-third
billion human beings, are divided into 500 million
Catholics and 450 million baptized non-Catholics, including Protestants, Orthodox, and Anglicans.

Polemic Dialogue

The first form of confrontation or dialogue that took
place between Christians was polemic in nature. I
shall try to define it, not by quoting a series of names
which would be of little interest, but by characteriz-
ing its method in a general way. This form first developed between Eastern and Western Christians in
the early centuries; then it sprang up again, this time
between Catholics and Protestants, during the Reformation.

To begin with, in a dispute of the polemic type,
immediate results are the aim. Nobody thinks—as I
shall later show to be the case with ecumenism—about
the historical dimensions involved. The times are not

taken into account, nor the effects on later centuries and on future generations. Instead, only immediate results are considered. For every objection there is a direct reply, and for each attack a counterattack. Sometimes also, every bad procedure is countered by another bad procedure.

Equally characteristic of this polemic era is the *immense value attributed to reasoning and authority,* to the way of intellectual persuasion. No one will ever find me disparaging intelligence, but today we know that intellectual reasons are not the only factors that enter into a man's convictions, and especially into his religious convictions. Many other psychological, sociological, historical, and emotional elements condition his attitudes and actions in fundamental ways. However, none of this was taken into account during the polemic era. And of course, the discovery of sociological conditioning and psychological processes, as well as the interest in these processes, is quite recent.

The third characteristic of the polemic method is what we may call the *atomization of the debate.* No one attempted to see the whole of his adversary's position, but only each particular point, and these were the subject of direct attack. The method itself was derived from the analytical procedure of medieval scholasticism. Long before Descartes, it used the Cartesian method of analysis, separating the difficulties and objections and considering each one in isolation. Inevitably, men who were trained in this method made use of it in the controversy of the early sixteenth century.

Thus we find them taking the difficulties one by one, without realizing that they actually formed a whole, and without seeking an interior coherence in an opponent's reasoning that would account for the details.

In this spirit, men prepared for debate with lists of errors. John Eck, a theologian (and by no means a negligible one) and a champion of Catholicism at the beginning of the Reformation, in 1530 came to the Diet of Augsburg at which the emperor was hoping to unite the two contending parties. Master Eck was armed with a list of 404 errors which he had found in Luther's teachings. But men did even better later on. The lists grew longer. There was that good Franciscan of the sixteenth century who called himself "Ardent Flame." He had discovered not merely 404 errors in Martin Luther, but 1,400! On the opposite side, of course, similar lists were compiled; indeed, there were whole books of lists. Nobody wondered what Luther was really trying to say or what had inspired the Reformation upheaval. Nobody was interested in the internal coherence or the spiritual import of the movement; no, they simply made lists of all the errors— partial, real, or supposed.

Under these circumstances, the controversy hardly progressed at all. None of the adversaries ever admitted any guilt on their part. Besides, is there ever a real meeting of minds by way of argument? Today we realize not only that the ideas of the Reformation and the East possess an internal cohesion which must be understood, if possible, in the light of this central point from which everything flows and everything is sustained, but also that Christian divisions, however different they may be—Eastern, German, Anglican—are not unrelated to each other, so that the problem of unity forms a whole which must be considered as such. Later we shall see this to be one of the essential features of the ecumenical movement.

The fourth characteristic of polemics is that *the arguments of the adversary are refuted, or at least are believed to be, without any thought of questioning one's own point of view.* One starts from positions considered as absolute, without making allowance for—let us not say "retreat," because we are not concerned with retreating but with advancing—going beyond the position actually held, and from which it would be possible to move ahead toward a fuller reality. This is the deplorable history of the controversies between East and West throughout the Middle Ages. They began in the ninth century, but unfortunately, continue into our own day, for the list is still unfinished. It has been a lamentable series of polemic writings in which the adversary is accused of everything that differs from one's own belief and practice. The Greeks reproach the Latins for not wearing beards. The Latins reproach the Greeks for not using holy oil in the ordination of priests. The Greeks accuse the Latins of having added the *Filioque* to the Creed—and indeed, the Latins did add the word—but one Latin theologian, and not a minor one either, accused the Greeks of having suppressed it, simply because they did not have it in the first place! Basically, no one had a high enough perception of the whole. Neither side was resourceful enough to interpret the other's position in a sufficiently broad perspective, or to consider the possibility of improving its own stand.

It is a fact that the sixteenth-century reformers, continental Protestants or Anglicans, never distinguished between the principles of Catholicism and the points that were only matters of detail or historical modalities. These distinctions should have been made; yet no one did so at the time because all were busy opposing each other point by point, never making any concessions and never questioning their own positions. Inevitably, the results were fatal: both sides only hardened their opposition. Arguing simply to win, finally culminates in upholding indefensible positions. The positions are defended because one has begun to argue, and that is all there is to it. To have learned one's catechism "against" someone is a great misfortune. We learned our catechism against Luther, and then against the Gallicans, against the modernists, against Kant, against Hegel, and against many others. The Protestants learned their catechism against the pope, against Bellarmine, against the Mass, and against the Virgin Mary. And the laity (in the French and ideological sense of the term) were educated against the ghosts of a rather remote past: against the Inquisition, against the *Sylabus,* against the temporal power of the papacy, and against clericalism. To be educated in *sed contra* is most unfortunate, because one's hands and feet are tied and there is no possibility of embracing truth in its fullness. But this does not mean that everything in the polemic method is bad. In the sixteenth century there were Catholic polemicists of great distinction. Their books contain not only true arguments, but also sometimes extremely interesting perceptions, as well as a certain freshness of outlook and broad approach to many questions. However, in order to indicate more clearly the progress made since then, I have presented the polemic method under its negative aspects.

Irenic Controversies

The era of bitter polemics led to nothing, and finally gave way to another approach. It was still a discussion, but an irenic one; that is to say, it was pursued in an attitude of spiritual serenity. It was disposed toward a better understanding of the other side and a better explanation of one's own. The most remarkable writer at this stage of the controversy was Bossuet, whose *Exposition of Catholic Doctrine* (1679) enjoyed immense success. He can teach us a great deal even today. Moreover, Bossuet (and less famous authors like the Jesuit, Veronius) understood well that, if the Protestants were opposed to the Catholic Church, it was not simply because of dogma. For even when the dogmatic basis was genuine, Protestants still refused to submit because of the forbidding superstructure of scholastic arguments which added precisions that the dogma itself neither needed nor imposed. That is why

Veronius, and after him Bossuet and many others, tried to present Catholicism in terms of its real and fundamental doctrines. They freed it from scholastic quarrels that were too subtle and arguable (because even among Catholics there can be differences of opinion), appealing instead to the Fathers, to common Tradition, and to the Councils as the surest criteria of authenticity. Furthermore, a certain effort is apparent in their writings to grasp the coherence of the Protestant position. In Bossuet this is evident: he acknowledged the internal coherence of Protestant attitudes. And although he denounced its contradictions, which have become clearer with the passage of time, he admitted that there was a real doctrinal construction in Protestantism resting upon a certain number of basic principles. This was progress; another step forward had been made.

Symbolism

During the eighteenth century there was a profound change of feeling. It began with a realization of the futility of any argument. Then, with the development of philosophy, the climate of the *aufklärung*, the Century of Enlightenment, more tolerant attitudes were adopted. To cite one example that I came across myself, a certain author of the eighteenth century, recopying a text of the previous century, replaced the words "errant brothers," which were always used in the seventeenth century, with the words "separated brothers," which we use today. This is a nuance, but it is a significant one.

At that time polemics, even irenic ones, were giving way to a more scientific form of exposition of the academic type. In some universities this new method became the subject of a teaching that went under the name of symbolism. The word requires explanation because it corresponds to nothing in our Catholic vocabulary. It refers to a Protestant practice. During the sixteenth century the Protestants, who were continuing the Reformation in many separate groups (Zwingli in Zurich; Calvin in France and Geneva; Bucer in Alsace; Luther in Saxony and Germany; etc.), began to feel the need of defining their professions of faith in documentary form. Some of these professions are famous. In France, for example, the fourth centennial of the *Confession of Faith of La Rochelle*, written by Calvin, was celebrated in 1960. Although certain of these documents were not strictly professions of faith—that is, lists of fairly short articles of belief—nevertheless they were accepted as authoritative, as was the case with Luther's *Little Catechism*, the *Augsburg Confession*, and the apology that followed it, etc. A list of all such documents that appeared during the eighteenth century alone would easily exceed fifty. They had the value of symbols of the faith, or creeds, in the Protestant Churches, in the same sense that we say the Credo is the symbol of our faith. When these documents were brought together in volumes, they formed a collection of "symbolical writings," a title by which Protestants still refer to them today. The idea occurred of making a statement of the positions of the various

Christian Churches by comparing the most valid of these documents, and the new scientific discipline was called "symbolical" or "creedal" theology.

The Protestants were the first to produce symbolical writings, and many Protestant names could be mentioned. Among the Catholics, by far the most celebrated was Jean-Adam Möhler, chief theologian of the Catholic school of Tübingen. I have a great personal devotion to this man who, unfortunately, died very young in 1838. We can still learn from Möhler today. The school of which he was the greatest exemplar might have saved us a century of research if it had been more closely followed, for by about 1830 it had developed practically everything that we are at present discovering in the realm of pastoral and kerygmatic methods.

However, the outlook of the symbolists was too narrow in one respect because, in considering the Protestant positions only from the viewpoint of their official texts, they committed the sin of academicism, even though their approach was honest and valid. A method may be excellent in the matter of studying texts, but it cannot be adequate for an approach to the being of another in its fullness. A text can never exhaust the position of a spirit. When it comes to a whole religious communion, this spiritual content overflows the intellectual plane and impregnates its life and its prayer—not only its private prayer, but also its liturgical prayer. And then it embodies itself in the collective behavior of a community that has its own particular genius and its own feeling, in the sense of *einfühlung*, that is, the penetration of an object from within.

The Konfessionskunde

Therefore it was most necessary that the symbolist writings should be complemented by a new approach that would come nearer to the concrete truth of the various religious positions. What value, for example, would an interpretation of Catholicism possess which was based exclusively on conciliar texts and on catechisms, with the addition of a bit of canon law and a few prayers or liturgical excerpts? There would be a fundamental difference between this wholly intellectual interpretation and a vital perception of Catholicism drawn from its living sources of prayer, meditation, and communal life.

This was the stage traversed during the second half of the nineteenth century as the accounts given by comparative symbolism were completed. Prepared from authentic texts, they provided a more concrete study of the religious attitudes, sociological groupings, ways of life, and prayer of Protestant Christians. A name has been given to this stage which, unfortunately, it is difficult to translate into other languages. The Germans call it *konfessionskunde,* meaning whatever acquaints us with the life of a denomination. Personally, I do not much care for the word "denomination" and almost always avoid it, because it too strongly suggests the strictly intellectual and legal aspects of the thing. I prefer to speak of "communion." To be sure, there is the word "church," but it is not always appropriate. It can be applied without objection in the case of Orthodox Christians, and in a descriptive sense for Protestants and Anglicans. In any case the word "communion," a religious term, goes beyond the too cerebral aspect of "denomination" and accentuates the living character of the prayer, the common liturgy and the concrete tradition of a Christian community.

A great step forward had been accomplished. Over and above the texts, thought was being given to the human realities that have played so large a part in dividing Christendom—a part so great that it might well be considered decisive. Without minimizing questions of doctrine, we are convinced of the determining significance in Christian divisions of anthropological differences and divergent cultural and social traditions, which are linked to history, geography, and many other elements. *Konfessionskunde*, at least in principle, embraces all these, and should include the developments permitted by the new techniques that currently have been placed at our disposal. Sociology in particular must be applied to the study of Christian divisions: it will certainly prove to be an extremely interesting field of research; and it is still awaiting not only its workers but even its pioneers, for the ground has hardly begun to be broken.

We have been describing the various steps of this progress in relationships, such as it has been, under the headings of polemics, irenic controversy, symbolist writings, and *konfessionskunde*. But now we have embarked upon a new stage, and have begun to write a new chapter.

The Ecumenical Advance

An eloquent symbol of this novel phenomenon is the creation of a new word. When a new word appears, its very appearance is an indisputable sign that a fresh reality has come to light. Although the adjective "ecumenical" has been known for a long time (it was used in classical Greek), it simply meant that which pertains to the *oikumene* or the inhabited earth. Anything that concerned the entire inhabited world was called ecumenical, and in practice this meant anything that concerned the Graeco-Roman Empire, the civilized region covered by Greek culture and later by Roman law. Such expressions as "ecumenical council" and "ecumenical patriarch" were used. But when, in 1920 or 1921, the substantive "ecumenism" was brought into being, a new reality was born.

Ecumenism incontestably represents a new reality in our present-day world. It is my conviction—and anyone who has the slightest contact with it is able to sense this—that the movement is born of God and has been brought to us by the Spirit of God. The distinguishing mark of a work of the Holy Spirit is the fact that realities or men, apparently not destined to meet, find themselves at a given moment led to co-operate toward a certain unity of action. It can be seen in religious foundations, in some forms of the apostolate, often in spite of contradictions and at times when it looks as though all is lost. When later on, one goes back over the past, it becomes apparent that many circumstances, some of which appeared to be thwarting it, were leading up to the event. The same thing is happening in the world of ecumenism, a world of Christians who are divided, but who believe that they are called by God to work together. At ecumenical meetings, it is the usual and almost classical thing to say, "The minute we meet together, Lutherans, Calvinists, Anglicans, Orthodox, Catholics, etc., we become heretics to one another." An ecumenical meeting is a meeting of believers who are heretics to one another. But in spite of their present irreducible oppositions, they are resolved to remain together in obedience to the call which they have heard.

Ecumenism, in relation to what we have previously said about the other stages of the Christian confrontation, is characterized primarily by the fact that *it embraces all the Christian divisions*. It does not belong merely to one chapter or one point in these divisions. The discovery has been made, not once but many times —and this is extremely significant—that, as soon as one aspect of ecumenism is touched upon, we are drawn into all its others. Typical of this is the example of the Chevetogne Foundation in Belgium. At first it was concerned with the Eastern Church exclusively, and there were some who wished to confine it to that sphere; however, this proved to be impossible. As soon as one element of the question is considered, all the others come with it: they comprise a whole.

Of course Orthodoxy is different from Protestantism; in some respects it is even more different from Catholicism. Nevertheless the Reformation might never have happened without the Eastern schism. There would have remained within Catholicism ferments of thought and a sense of transcendence that the devotional and even the theological developments of the Middle Ages have hidden from our view. Everything is integral, and ecumenism looks at the whole. Regardless of the differences between the East and Germany or England, divided Christendom possesses a certain unity.

Even more characteristic of the movement is the fact of *seeing the positive Christianity in others,* and not just the negative. Consequently the Protestant is not simply one who refuses to recognize the supremacy of the pope, who denies five sacraments out of seven, who refuses to recognize the Virgin Mary, but is a Christian who lives by many positive values in Christianity, and who, ever since the sixteenth century, has been developing these values in his prayers, study, and thought. But with numerous errors? No doubt; nevertheless they have their positive aspects, including missionary activity, Christian witness, and a variety of initiatives. Only someone who has experienced these things can speak of them with full knowledge: one has to make the "ecumenical experiment." One has to have met a Christian of another communion, have prayed with him, have seen his faith in Jesus Christ and been moved by it, have discovered, in a word, that one can receive something from him. How much better this is than attacking the 404 or the 1,400 errors of Luther!

Characteristic also of ecumenism is *a search for plenitude.* Instead of looking for opposition and jealously keeping whatever is distinctive, ecumenism has within it a desire for catholicity. The thing that makes a heresy is not so much the error as what theologians call pertinacity. If the heretic is of good faith and willing to correct himself, there is no heresy; heresy requires stubbornness and hardening. To the extent, for example, that modern Protestantism sees the excessive particularism of its opposition to Catholics and tries to overcome it, it is not heretical. In its attachment to the Bible, it has become too set *against* tradition and *against* the Magisterium; this it recognizes, and to that extent carries within itself a desire for catholicity and plenitude, admitting that the Scriptures are not everything, but must be read in the framework of a tradition. This becomes very evident in the ecumenical movement; the Protestants taking part in it refer to the Scriptures, and yet they are not in complete agreement. Why? Because they too read Scripture according to a certain tradition, and therefore the word "only" in the formula "the Bible *only,*" should not be there.

A final trait that characterizes the ecumenical movement is that *ecumenism works on the scale of history.* Polemics are good enough for opposing argument with argument; it only takes a few hours. For the plenitude that ecumenism requires, however, a maturation is necessary which involves long periods of time. A man who acquires three true ideas in a year—and by that I mean a fertile seed within the mind, a principle of understanding in the domain of the real—has not wasted his time. And in the divisions between us and our separated brethren we are dealing with inveterate habits: religious attitudes anchored in the depths of consciousness! It takes time to move this religious certitude even a few degrees around its axis. This is all the more true because a soul is never solitary; it belongs to a Church, to a whole communion. We have to think in terms of generations and centuries. But ecumenism is working on the historical scale. Two excellent texts on this subject are enlightening, although neither was written with ecumenism in view. The first is by Cardinal Newman, who was sixty-two years old when he wrote in a letter: "What I aim at is not immediate conversions, but to influence, as far as an old man can, the tone of thought in the place, with a view to a distant time when I shall no longer be here." The historical dimension is plain to see: Newman's goal is not immediate. Controversy might have brought about conversions at once. But he preferred to influence ways of thinking in England and the world many years after his death. He was sowing, and looking ahead to the time of germination and flowering.

The second text is by Etienne Gilson. It was written on the subject of controversies between schools of philosophy, but it applies very well to the theme of ecumenism. "When their conclusions are opposite, adversaries must be given the necessary time to understand one another better, to understand themselves better, and so to meet at a still undetermined point which is certainly situated beyond their present positions." This is what is meant by working on an historical scale, because so often we have been divided over misunderstandings. The proof of this is that the first subject of discord between the East and the West was the question of the Holy Spirit, the *Filioque*, in the time of Photius (ninth century). Today it is recognized that, correctly explained, this point did not justify a separation.

For Protestantism, a similar point of doctrinal obscurity would be the question of justification by faith. A few years ago a German-Swiss priest, Hans Küng, wrote a thesis on justification in the writings of Karl Barth. In his thesis he showed that Barth and the Council of Trent may be reconciled and may even coincide. He requested Karl Barth himself to write a preface for him. Barth answered: "In the first place, you have understood me very well; that is my position. Secondly, if what you say about the Council of Trent is true, I declare that I have no objections, and am ready to come to Trent in penitential garb and say to the Fathers: *Patres, peccavi.*" And it was over justification that they separated in the sixteenth century! We are not staking everything on this one thesis, and there is still matter for discussion. But at least a door has been opened which was barred and bolted before. By having the patience to explain ourselves better to one another, and also to explain ourselves better to ourselves, it is possible to find the road that leads to reconciliation. We too must thoroughly examine points of doctrine concerning the papacy, the Church, the Eucharist, etc. That is the ecumenical attitude.

What are the best ways of achieving it? I shall sum them up under four main headings. The first way is *resourcement*—going back to the sources. Beyond the streams which run between the revelation of Jesus Christ and ourselves, we must find our way back to the true source to which the Holy Scriptures bear witness: the Holy Scriptures that we can never separate from the way in which they are read by the people of God, that is to say, from Tradition. We must center our thought once more on the altar instead of remaining in the side chapels, and it must be centered on the unique mystery of the liturgical year, which is Easter. Examining the Scriptures, the Fathers, and the liturgy, we reach two apparently conflicting results: plenitude and purity both at once. Their antinomy often arises in the sense that the greater the plenitude we seek, the greater is the risk of amalgamating disparate elements and thus losing purity. If, on the other hand, we seek the purity of the message, we are applying our minds to one of its values alone, and neglecting the context which constitutes its plenitude. When I go back to the sources, I find that there is more in the Holy Scriptures than all that we have been able to draw from them thus far! The source ever remains more powerful than the streams, and we find the ancient proverb true: *Fons vincit sitientem* ("The spring is greater than the drinker's thirst"). When we go back to the sources and drink more deeply than before, when we submit our lives and thoughts to the discipline of the Holy Scriptures, we become different men, stronger in life, more assured of ourselves, more open to others, and more unified. Protestants, who have studied the Bible so deeply and have published whole libraries of books about it, go on delving into it just the same and discover treasures in it that they did not know before. The results of Protestant exegesis today are drawing perceptibly closer to those of Catholic exegesis. The authors are reading and quoting one another. Going back to the sources makes it possible to bypass positions that are too inflexible or too narrow, to separate the original content from the afflux of later creations.

To go back to the sources is not enough: there must be *dialogue* as well. What we have to receive from one another is not a truth that we may not have possessed, because the Church, ideally understood, is perfect. But that is just it: the Church has never been ideally understood, and has never throughout her long history been perfectly realized. The actual Church of today or of any day needs to be given at least a shake-up. And this shaking-up is being brought about by the ecumenical movement. In prewar ecumenism—and the formula is still valid for postwar ecumenism—a question was put as much to Protestants as to Catholics: "Have you taken seriously such or such an element that is part of your faith?" The Protestants would say to us: "Have you taken seriously the free gift of the grace of God? the gravity of sin? Have you taken seriously the uniqueness of the Mediator, Jesus Christ?" And we would say to the Protestants: "Have you taken seriously the real unity of the Church, the continuity and the apostolicity of the ministry? Have you taken seriously the reality of the Mystical Body which makes us members of that Body and the communion of saints which authorizes the community of prayer and veneration?" In such a dialogue it is important to keep clear of hasty apologetics and to give oneself the time to understand the different positions. To enter into a great doctrine demands years of effort if it is to be penetrated completely; polemics seem quick and easy by comparison. The ecumenical effort itself is a progressive entering into plenitude and purity, through an approach to the sources, under the shock of dialogue. It needs time. To understand certain environments, one must go right into them and live in them for a long time; that is the experience we have undergone. Nobody can claim, in any environment whatsoever, to be able to master his own psychology or his deepest reactions, *a fortiori,* because things are still more complicated in the world of separated Christians.

The third element is *history.* History gives us the immense advantage of being able to distinguish the absolute from the relative. Without historical education in fact, there is no discernment (one might believe, for example, that St. Peter wore a white cassock and a pectoral cross, like the pope wears today). In reality all the essential things exist under historical forms and modalities. It is all the more important to realize this because, in the sixteenth century—and it was exactly the same in the eleventh century where the East was concerned—no one made any distinctions. The Protestants totally rejected the Mass because the candles, or some prayer or other, displeased them. They threw out the whole thing, the baby and the bathwater.

Nowadays we have a better understanding of the complexity of reality, and we can more clearly discern the essential doctrines from the historical modalities which appeared at a particular time. That is important for understanding the reforms of the sixteenth century, which amounted to a global rejection of the Church—apparently with good reason. History had disfigured the face of the Church, accentuating certain traits like the growth of the temporal power of the papacy. But the Reformation did not make the necessary distinctions; in the papal power it failed to distinguish what was merely an historical excrescence related to the public laws of that epoch of Christianity from what was essentially Christian. And the same is true with regard to other domains.

Finally, the fourth element of ecumenism is *spiritual*. This element does not answer to a concern for edification; rather, it is in the deepest nature of things. For ecumenism is not an academic or diplomatic activity, but is an essentially Christian one, like the apostolate or the missions. Souls are committed to it in accordance with their attitudes of faith, of love, of prayer, and of mutual service. A chapter of the history of salvation is being brought into reality, not a chapter of secular history; and for this, prayer is the first and most precious of conditions. Its first effect is to purify our hearts, a condition that is absolutely necessary. The work of ecumenism is not intellectual juggling, a matter of competence or *savoir faire*; it requires a deep conversion of the heart of a man, and of all his Christian activity. And prayer has the virtue, if it be true prayer, of reforming the mind and heart. A second condition, as we know from experience, and from a strictly intellectual perspective to which sooner or later we must come, is the level that prayer enables us to reach that we could not otherwise attain. This level is the plateau of confrontation, of discussion, of exchange, of dialogue. Very often it happened during discussions with our separated brethren, that the dialogue seemed to have reached a ceiling, or was leading to an impasse; and then the way opened again as a result of intense and prolonged prayer together. This took place, not by an abdication of intelligence in favor of feeling or enthusiasm, but at the intellectual level itself: the eyes that did not see had been opened.

Ecumenism is all of these things together: it is a return to the sources, with the exegetical means which are available to us today; it is a dialogue, with all that this implies in the way of familiarity with foreign languages, conferences, human availability, and the knowledge of the past which is history; it is prayer; in a word, it is a living and rich synthesis in which there is a realization of the ideal conditions for that objective, so greatly to be desired, which we may evoke in closing in terms of a union of purity and plenitude.

2

The Christian Conscience and the Problem of Reunion and Ecumenism *

The occasion of this gathering assumes for me a special solemnity. For almost twenty years I have been making lecture tours in France and the neighboring countries during the Week of Universal Prayer for Unity. This time, I wanted to come to the East, because this year we are celebrating an anniversary *together*: you have already guessed that I am speaking of the schism of 1054.

Since then, there have been several attempts at reunion. At the Council of Lyons in 1274—it failed for lack of moral and theological preparation—Pope Gregory X began his address with the tender and moving words of our Lord: "I have desired with a great desire to eat this passover with you" (Luke 22:15). I too have desired with a great desire to eat with you this passover that we are going to celebrate this evening. Alas, it is not, and it cannot yet be, the Eucharistic passover. But it can be, and will be, a passover of sincerity and truth such as the Apostle Paul spoke of. According to the

*An address delivered at Athens in January of 1954.

39

sixth chapter of John, there are two forms of the Bread of Life: first, the Eucharistic bread, and then the bread of the word and of truth. We can prepare ourselves to partake of the one by partaking of the other.

The schism of the eleventh century between the East and the West broke, as it were, the transverse bar of the cross. A second great rupture, that of the sixteenth century, broke its vertical bar, splitting Christianity from North to South. We may very well suppose that this second split would not have happened if the first had been avoided and if the ferments of Eastern thought had remained active in the ecclesiastical life of the West.

Thus we find ourselves faced with a divided Christian world. There is the Catholic block with perhaps 450 to 500 million faithful. (The figures are quite approximate, and are given only to emphasize the separation of the different Christian groups.) There are all the Protestants, some 220 million souls, divided not merely into the great families of the Reformation, but also into many sects (in the United States, there are 45 denominations with more than 50,000 members each, and over 200 with less than 50,000 each). Then there is the huge Orthodox family, whose numbers are difficult to estimate because of the unknown presented to us by the vastness of Russia. For our purposes, however, let us say that they comprise between 150 and 170 million baptized members. Finally, there are the Anglicans, with 45 to 50 million baptized members.

This division of those who profess to be disciples of Jesus Christ is a scandal. A scandal, first, because there is one God, one Savior, Jesus Christ, and one baptism! The scandal was brought home to me when an American delegate at Amsterdam in 1948 said with sad humor, "And now we are going to pray for the Brides of Jesus Christ." The Brides of Jesus Christ! As though there could be several! An eloquent symbol of our divisions is the Holy Sepulchre at Jerusalem. The Holy Sepulchre is falling into ruin, and we are incapable of repairing it because we cannot agree. From time to time arguments arise there, because the Greeks have encroached by one yard on the Latin chapel, or because the Latins have encroached by a quarter of an hour on the Greek timetable! And then uniformed Moslem soldiers have to leave the divan on which they are lying to come and restore peace among the Christians!

The scandal of division is felt even more strongly in the mission field. Imagine a Chinese or an African watching the approach of about a dozen different missionaries—Methodist, Anglican, Catholic—each one inviting him to receive his baptism. And so it was from the missionary world, especially from the Protestant and American missions, that the impulse came which resulted in the Ecumenical Movement. If we had to fix a precise date for the birth of the Ecumenical Movement, it would be 1910, the year in which the World Assembly of Protestant Missions took place at Edinburgh.

To begin with, the movement took two forms, which arose from two different preoccupations, or perhaps one might say from two different spiritual families. Some people were concerned chiefly with practical action: they centered their efforts around the Life and Work Movement. Others are preoccupied with questions of principles and problems in the Church, and they began the Faith and Order Movement. But the concerns of the two movements became sufficiently identical, under the influence of various factors, for a fusion into a single organization whose title was to be decided upon in 1938. The war delayed its realization; hence at the Conference of Amsterdam in 1948 the new organization was officially constituted under the title of The World Council of Churches.

This is not a very fortunate name: it suggests the idea of a directive organization, and also of grave discussions around a felt-covered table. The Greek form of it is more accurate: *Koinonia tôn Ekklesiôn.* The Council is in no way a super-Church, with authority over the others; nor is it a reunited Church. Alas, it is much more. As an Orthodox delegate said, it is like an assemblage of heretics. It is a gathering of men who are heretics for each other: for the Orthodox, a Calvinist is a heretic; for a Lutheran, the Orthodox are heretics. But these men, heretics for one another, are conscious of having a common work to do. The Amsterdam Conference of 1948 ended with the slogan, "We intend to stay together." The World Council is an assembly of divided Christians who intend to seek together ways of reconciliation and, if the grace is given them, of unity. It is the place where the delegates of the member-Churches try to live out their obedience to the call they have felt toward union. It is the means for their dialogue, the setting for their mutual aid, and the place, finally, where they strive to produce a common witness to Jesus Christ before the world.

This year of 1954 is not only that of the ninth centenary of the breach between the East and the West, centering about Rome. It will also witness a great assembly of the World Council of Churches at Evanston, near Chicago, on the theme of "Jesus Christ, the Hope of the World." And here I want very sincerely to salute this gigantic effort. I want to bear witness to the sincerity and selflessness of the men who are working in the Ecumenical Movement. I like to think that all this has a meaning in the plan of God, who so often "writes straight with crooked lines," as a Portuguese proverb says. I was delighted to learn that the Holy Synod of the Greek Orthodox Church had decided to send such a brilliant delegation to the Evanston Conference.

However, at this conference, as at the preceding ones, the Catholic Church will be officially absent. From the beginning, in fact, she has refused to participate as a member of the movement, which is Protestant in origin and includes all the Christian communities except herself. What can be the motives for this refusal?

Sometimes people speak of the pride that would prevent the Catholic Church from sitting down as a sister among others at the council table. It is not a question of pride, but of fidelity to what the Catholic Church has received the vocation and the grace to be. The first motive is of a doctrinal order. She cannot act as though the unity of the Church of Christ and of the Apostles was an open question, or something still to be found. She could not willingly enter a movement whose central purpose is the search for that unity. If the unity of the Church of Christ and of the Apostles had ever been lost, nothing and no one could restore it. It is unthinkable that it does not exist today in the world, visible to those who have eyes to see, and that it has not existed continuously since the Cross and the Last Supper, right down through history. Therefore unity is not something yet to be achieved, but rather to be recognized; and once recognized, there can be no question but of meeting *there*. Fundamentally, union can only be a reunion within the Church.

This doctrinal theme of the Catholic Church is as valid as ever. Meanwhile, however, the Ecumenical Movement has been considerably deepened and purified; it no longer has the pragmatic and liberal character of the 1920's; today there would be nothing to prevent a Church from taking part in it even while affirming herself to be *the* true Church of Jesus Christ. Is not that precisely the position of the Orthodox Churches? But the Catholic Church has still other motives, of a pastoral order, for not participating officially in the Ecumenical Movement and its conferences. It is hard to imagine a large body like the Catholic Church engaging in such an uncertain and poorly-defined movement. Rome in particular likes things to be definite, and feels uneasy in the face of an assem-

blage that has such shaky foundations and such un-
clear goals. What would be understood, for example,
in the World Council of Churches, by the divinity of
Jesus Christ? by the Holy Trinity? And then, above
all, the Catholic Church is afraid of giving credit among
the faithful to the idea that she would be prepared to
make concessions, not merely on practical points but on
points of doctrine. She is afraid of encouraging a kind
of dogmatic indifferentism toward which many people
are already inclined ("All religions are equally good"),
and which experience shows to be the first step toward
practical atheism.

But, if the Catholic Church has not participated
officially in the Ecumenical Movement, it has not been
for lack of interest. The movement has been followed
in prayer. A very large number of the faithful, including priests and theologians, keep themselves well
informed about the activities of the World Council.
The Council's Secretary General, Mr. Visser 't Hooft,
said at the time of the Amsterdam Conference (1948)
that the great fact, the great revelation, had been the
active interest shown by the Catholics. Moreover,
there are many groups, in almost every country, which
hold regular meetings with Protestants, Orthodox, and
Anglicans. These meetings are not of an official kind,
but they are followed and approved by the bishops, and
eventually even by the Holy See. And finally, over the
whole range of theological problems, there has been
a general reopening of dialogue with our separated
brethren. This is happening in books as well as in

conversations. It is a fact that we are reading non-Catholic authors and are taking account of their questions and their contributions, just as they are opening themselves to ours.

The result of all this is that we cannot avoid taking an attitude with regard to ecumenism, and that, if our attitude is a positive one and not purely critical, we shall have to put forward an exact declaration and a justification of our position. This is what I want to do very quickly.

You will understand, from what I have already said, that we shall always think of reunion taking place within the Church of Christ and of the Apostles. I will tell you later under what conditions we can envisage this when it comes to the Orthodox Churches.

There are two possible roads to reunion. We can try to reunite one or another individual, straight away, to the Church exactly as it is. This is a matter of individual passage, or, if we are not afraid of the word, of conversion. I must say here that the Church has always admitted this, and that there can be no objection to it, on one condition: that the spiritual freedom of all concerned has been fully respected. Every Church does it in any case; but, although this may be the solution for one soul, it is just as clear that it cannot be the solution when we are looking at the problem of Christian reunion as a whole, or if we are "bitten" by the ecumenical problem as such.

The appearance of a new word is always the sign that a new reality has come to light. When Auguste

Comte created the word "sociology" around 1840, or when the word "proletarian" appeared for the first time in French in 1817, it was because new social realities had come into being as a result of the Industrial Revolution of the eighteenth century. There has always been a desire for Christian reunion, and there is nothing new about the adjective "ecumenical." But when the noun "ecumenism" appeared about 1920, in the world of divided Christians, it was because a new activity with reunion in view had begun to make headway. We were passing from the level of narrowly individual work to that of a common endeavor, which is now being carried out on the scale of history. There is a text of Newman's that expresses my thought remarkably well: "What I aim at is not immediate conversions, but to influence, as far as an old man can, the tone of thought in the place, with a view to a distant time when I shall no longer be here."

Newman was speaking not only of Anglicans. He wanted to influence ways of thinking in England, and he was including the Catholics. Newman was a genius and a famous writer. But I, who am only a simple man, would like to take up his text again by saying, "I want to influence the ways of thinking of *the world!*" Yes, of the world! Why not, if it is true that an idea expressed in Paris is known forty-eight hours afterwards in Buenos Aires, and on the same day in Athens? With communications as they are today, and with the frontiers of denominational particularism having been so often attacked, one can really hope to influence the whole world little by little, like the circles in a pond, especially since one is not working alone. Everybody works according to his ability, but others alongside are doing similar work; and above all there are other Christians, belonging to other communions, who are somehow coming to meet us, even if they have started from very far away.

This working on the scale of history is also, or is trying to be, a work of convergence. And as I was just now expressing myself through the pen of Cardinal Newman, I would also like to borrow the words of a Catholic philosopher, Etienne Gilson. This is what he wrote: "When their conclusions are opposite, adversaries must be given the necessary time to understand one another better, to understand themselves better, and so to meet at a still undetermined point which is certainly situated beyond their present positions." This text puts us on the road to the solution of an antinomy that seems to be written at the heart of all ecumenical work: we must change; and we cannot change. We must change because, if we do not change things nothing will happen. We shall be in the same situation in another two thousand years, if there are still any Christians left in the world, looking at each other from a distance like cats watching one another and showing their claws. And yet, nobody can ask any one of us to give up what he holds to be true in his own Church.

To change and not to change: there is a solution to this antinomy and it is called development. Coming home on vacation at the end of a school year, we have all heard our mothers say, "My, how you've changed!" And yet, we were really the same. An Anglican author once wrote the same thing about the Catholic Church: "She cannot change, but she can explain." For my part I am convinced that many things which are thought of as dividing us now are capable of being explained in such a way that the possibility of maintaining or re-establishing communion would become apparent.

This is not a supposition; it is a fact. For centuries, the question of the Procession of the Holy Spirit has been held up among us as an insurmountable cause of separation. Today, thanks to a number of honest explanations and careful historical research, a great many Catholic and Orthodox theologians believe that— provided there is a willingness to accept a favorable interpretation, but one that respects what must be respected on both sides—there is no justification here for remaining divided. And what are we to say about those really ridiculous polemic themes that have managed to play such an important part down through the centuries: questions of the beard, the Alleluia, the Saturday fast, and all the rest? Who would dare to divide the members of Christ over these today?

But, if we have been able to explain ourselves on points that for so long have appeared to be devisive, in such a way as to create the possibility of understanding, why can it not be done, now and in the future, over those that still divide us, and particularly the one which is the main issue at present, the question of the Roman primacy? I am convinced that there is ground to be cleared and gained on this point by honest biblical, historical, and theological research. I am convinced that we could arrive at common conclusions concerning what Catholic apologetics claims and what the Orthodox position admits.

Such a development toward a point of convergence brings into play two great means which, with the addition of a third, are the main instruments of the worker for union: dialogue and *resourcement*.

Dialogue has two major enemies, monologue and confusion. Confusion exists when everyone speaks anarchically and without expressing a firm position. As for monologue, it is the very opposite of dialogue, which supposes that we shall also listen to others, be open to the questions they ask us, and be ready to take them seriously. Dialogue has the immense benefit of dissipating prejudice and correcting false interpretations. Often we are opposed because we do not know each other; and we do not know each other because we do not associate with or talk to each other. Besides, dialogue is rather like prayer: we may not get what we are asking for, but real prayer always has the effect of making us better *in ourselves*. Hence we do not come out of dialogue exactly the same as we went in. We have met a brother, and we have made ourselves a brotherly heart. There will be some things that we shall no longer be able to say or think about the other, or at least that we shall not say or think in the same way.

By *resourcement* I mean a return to the deep springs, a reinterrogation of the sources which are essentially the Scriptures, the Fathers, and the liturgy. There are two ways of being Catholic, and also, I think, of being Orthodox. We can stubbornly cling to the letter of the positions of our own Church and try to justify them at all costs; or we can revitalize the present positions of our Church in contact with the great sources which are common to all of us. Divergences will remain, but they will be differences rather than oppositions. We shall remain faithful to our own Church; our loyalty will be even greater and stronger than it was before. But it will be in a spirit that has reached a higher understanding of things, far above the petty rivalries of letter against letter and justification against justification.

Ecumenism implies a sane and true reformation. In an activity of this nature the part of the layman is essential. Thanks to the shock or to the impulse generated by ecumenical dialogue we are now having to move forward on all fronts, on the other side and *on our own*, in such a way that we are all advancing toward the still undetermined point of convergence situated beyond our present positions and oppositions. It will be, if God wills, a point of reunion. Catholic dogma leads us to believe only one thing: the Catholic Church will not have to change her essential line of development in order to realize that the point of convergence lies on the trajectory of her history.

A few moments ago I suggested a supplementary condition. I would not want it to have the appearance of being an afterthought. I was thinking of it from the first. All this endeavor must not be only intellectual and cerebral. It must be pursued in a religious atmosphere. We approach our brothers, and we approach these subjects too, in different ways when we come to them as scholars or as Christians, by which I mean men of religion. We can pass through the door of ecumenism only on our knees. And here I cannot help remembering the saintly figure of Abbé Paul Couturier, who died in 1953. He was the apostle of the Universal Week of Prayer for Unity, which takes place each year from January the eighteenth to the twenty-fifth. He gave to our Catholic ecumenical work the whole of its spiritual dimension. He gave it its heart of prayer. His formula was one that we could all adopt: The unity that God wills, in the way that he wills.

In closing, I would like to tell you a story with a moral. It is taken from the life of a Swiss saint of the fifteenth century, Nicolas de Flue. He was the father of eleven children. He heard the call to a hermit's life and retired to a lonely valley. But he seemed to be like the spirit of unity of the Swiss Confederation, and people came to consult him from all the various cantons. One day, some cantons that were on the point of declaring war sent delegates to him to explain their quarrel. Nicolas took his cord, made a knot in it and held it out to the delegates, saying, "Will you untie this knot?" They did it easily. "That is the way," said the saint, "that the difficulties of men must be untangled." When the delegates protested that it was not so easy, Nicolas answered, "You would not have been able to undo the cord either, if we had both been pulling against each other."

3

The World Council of Churches

At the end of November and the beginning of December, 1961, the third assembly of the World Council of Churches took place in New Delhi. The press gave it considerable publicity, and even the general public showed great interest. The preceding meetings had taken place at Amsterdam in 1948, and Evanston, Illinois, in 1954. What exactly does the World Council of Churches represent? How did it originate, what are its dynamics, and in which direction is it moving? This is what I now propose to examine, so that we can arrive at an understanding of the depth, the greatness, the interest, and the hope of the Ecumenical Movement.

Let us make it clear first of all that the expression "Ecumenical Movement" is open to two interpretations. In one sense we can say that the Ecumenical Movement includes everything that is being done everywhere to bring Christians together and to encourage them to reunite in a visible unity as disciples of Jesus Christ. In this broad sense, Catholics are taking part in it, and were actively doing so long before the movement existed in its narrower connotation. One could cite the names of many pioneers of the nineteenth century and the early years of the twentieth. Think, for example, of Father Portal, of Dom Lambert Baudouin, of Cardinal Mercier, who were most active agents in the Ecumenical Movement in its broad conception. Here, however, we are concerned with the Ecumenical Movement, not in a narrow sense—one could hardly call a work of such breadth "narrow"—but in the stricter sense in which it designates a movement that embodies Christians, without the official participation of the Catholic Church, in the organization called the World Council of Churches.

To understand the birth of the movement, we must look back into the past and remind ourselves of the situation of Protestantism in the nineteenth century.

The Protestantism of the sixteenth century was not of a missionary nature. Individuals and small groups did send missionaries abroad, of course, but the great Protestant communions, the Calvinists, the Lutherans, and the Anglicans, did not. These did not begin to move until much later. A few missionary foundations made their appearance in the seventeenth century; by the end of the eighteenth century they were more numerous. However, not until the nineteenth century, with the colonial penetration of the Western powers into Africa, Asia, and the South Seas, did Protestant missions begin to develop with the extraordinary intensity with which we are familiar. Yet their development took place under conditions totally different from those of the Catholic missions. We Catholics are accustomed to thinking of missions within the clearly-defined structure of the Church: missionaries belong to orders of men or women, or to diocesan or national organizations; all of these are supervised in one way or another by the pope as supreme head of the Catholic Church. Catholic missions are essentially a Church undertaking. The Protestant missions, on the other hand, were not always sent out by organized Churches. In many cases they were the result of private initiative, or of societies founded by an individual. A minister, for example, who had been moved by the situation that he had encountered in visiting some part of Africa, would come back home, collect funds, and found a missionary organization, often under his own name. Protestant missionary expansion came about, therefore, not exactly in an anarchic fashion, but certainly in dispersed order. The organization and distribution of its efforts were not centrally planned. This again reflected the internal divisions of the families which originated with the Reformation. The Anglicans, the Lutherans, and the Methodists were evangelizing the pagan world side-by-side.*

The nineteenth century, which witnessed this phase of Protestant missionary expansion, also saw the beginnings of reorganization. From 1850 onward, a large

---

*This situation reflects the basic difference between Catholic and Protestant concepts of the structure of the Church. Early Protestant missionary endeavors were church-related more through their personnel rather than through a central organization like the Congregation for the Propagation of the Faith. [Editor's note]

number of Lutheran, Calvinist, and other federations were founded. In the student world, notably, there were associations of Christian students—the Student Christian Movement, and the World Federation of Student Christian Movements—dominated from the start by two aspirations: the missionary aspiration, and that of regroupment. Each of these aspirations was to become an extremely powerful factor of union and fusion.

It was in this climate, and with the aim of drawing together, that a conference of all the Protestant missions took place at Edinburgh in 1910. There is general agreement today that the birth of the Ecumenical Movement dates from this conference. An incident, quite small in appearance, gave the impetus to the whole series of events that have occurred since then in an accelerating rhythm. Toward the end of the conference, one of the Far Eastern delegates—his name is unrecorded, and he remains among those anonymous figures of history who accomplish great things without realizing it—stood up and spoke to the congress just as it was beginning to disperse. "You have sent us missionaries who have taught us to know Jesus Christ, and we thank you for that. But you have also brought us your divisions. Some of you preach Lutheranism, others Methodism, or Congregationalism, or Episcopalianism. We ask you to preach us the Gospel, and to allow Jesus Christ himself to arouse in the hearts of our peoples, by the action of his Holy Spirit, a Church which conforms to his demands and will conform also to the spirit of our different races. It will be the Church of Christ in Japan, the Church of Christ in China, the Church of Christ in India, delivered from all the 'isms' that you have inflicted on us in your preaching of the Gospel." This declaration made a very deep impression on the assembly, and particularly on Charles Brent who was a clergyman of the Episcopalian Church in America. He was haunted by the thought. Shortly after returning home he told his friends and followers of his intention to find some remedy for the situation of disunity among Christians. To answer the urgent missionary needs of the unevangelized peoples, they would have to preach one Gospel.

Charles Brent launched a movement which soon took the name of Faith and Constitution, or Faith and Order, because it was centered on doctrinal questions: questions about the Church, the sacraments, the priesthood, and ecclesiastical organizations. Almost at the same time a slightly different, but parallel, movement came into being in response to the needs of spirits less preoccupied with ideas and more with action. It was called Life and Work, and very soon had as its principal promoter the Lutheran Archbishop of Upsala, Dr. Nathan Söderblom. These were the years 1910-1911; Europe was calm, and it was then that the first chapter of the history of the Ecumenical Movement began to be written—the chapter I have attempted to retrace in my book *Chrétiens désunis,* which was published in 1937. Since then, a second chapter, very different from the first, has been begun. We are living through it now, and the New Delhi conference marks one of its paragraphs. The story of this second chapter has been told by Father Le Guillou in *Mission et Unité*.

I shall be returning in a moment to the second chapter of ecumenical history, but before doing so I should like to describe the general aspects—spiritual, intellectual, and moral—of the first, that of the years 1910-1937.

Following the interruption of the First World War, Life and Work resumed its activities after the armistice and was able to hold its first general conference at Stockholm in 1925. The Faith and Order movement held its own first conference at Lausanne in 1927. Certainly there were considerable differences between the two movements: the latter was more concerned with ideas and doctrine; the former had a greater attachment to practical problems, seeking to give a Christian answer to the great human dramas of war, hunger, alcoholism, slavery, slums. In reality, however, both were working more or less along the same lines.

You will understand me better if I give you a picture which is easy to remember and, I think, accurate. Imagine a flat, horizontal surface, and place on it the separated Christian communities: Anglicanism, the various denominations of Protestantism, and Eastern Orthodoxy (insofar as the Orthodox Churches were already then taking part in the Ecumenical Movement). The problem was seen at that time as a confrontation of doctrinal positions on the horizontal plane, and an attempt to make them coincide as far as possible. Wherever divergences appeared, there were efforts to explain and to clarify the various positions. Through these exchanges, it was hoped to extend the "surface of agreement" and to reach a formula that everyone could adopt. Finally, at least on those particular points, there was no longer any reason for remaining divided. In fact, it was rather like a jigsaw puzzle, if I may be permitted the comparison, in which the different pieces must be fitted one into another so that the bulges correspond with the hollows, and one tries by searching for the secret of their arrangement to rebuild the original picture. It was a question, then, of a comparison between the various positions of the Churches, of a discussion between Church and Church in which, starting from the actual division, there were efforts to meet together and reach, as far as possible, unanimity on certain points either of doctrine (Trinity, Eucharist, Christology, sacraments), or of practice (ecclesiastical life, organization of worship, the priesthood).

However, by the time the next conferences were due to be held, in 1937, the general world climate had evolved profoundly. The economic crisis had spread from the United States to the whole world; there had been outbreaks of persecution against Catholics here and there, notably in Mexico; and the Protestants, who were abandoning nineteenth-century liberal optimism with its primary interest in man, were joining the school of Karl Barth, and were beginning once more to read and publish works on God and theology. Above all, there had intervened a political event of which it is difficult to exaggerate the importance: the rise to power of Hitler in January of 1933. The new regime showed itself to be fundamentally a-Christian and even anti-Christian. Its advances toward the Churches had no other aim but to cajole them so as better to tame them.

This is not the place to describe the Catholic resistance; however, the nature of the Protestant resistance must be recalled. It finally grouped itself about Karl Barth, although he was not the only leader. Faced with Hitler's attempt to dominate the Church and use it for his own ends, an active group, united under the name of the "Confessing Church," sprang up and proclaimed that the Church recognized only one Savior, Jesus Christ. The group declared itself ready to obey him, even if it meant disobeying the established government. The Confessing Church was thus vigorously opposed to the Nazi ideology, which a compliant bishop, Dr. Müller, was attempting to spread throughout the Reich.

At first sight it may seem that, by taking this stand for a transcendent reason—the Lordship of Jesus Christ, who is in Heaven—these men would have to break away from politics and give up the hope of any immediate effectiveness. Exactly the reverse happened. Their stand gave them an incomparable political effectiveness, even if it was to prove burdensome for them. When their sole concern had been to obey their Lord in Heaven, it was given to them to present to the world, and above all to their own countrymen, an authentically Christian witness, and, moreover, to find themselves united in this witness and this fidelity. These men came from very different backgrounds: from Lutheranism, from Calvinism, or from the intermediate Church which was created in 1817 by the King of Prussia, the "United Church" of which Pastor Niemöller was a member. But, in the Confessing Church, there were no more Lutherans, Calvinists, or "Uniteds"; there were nothing but faithful followers of the Gospel who, by the power of their obedience to Jesus Christ, had been brought together in the exercise of their responsibility toward the world. They proclaimed a message of Christian worth, at the same time receiving the gift of finding themselves united. The experience they underwent at that time was decisive for the Protestants, and showed them the path they would have to follow from then onwards in their quest for unity.

In 1937, when the two movements, Faith and Order and Life and Work, decided to hold their second world assemblies, they had drawn sufficiently close to be able to organize them in the same year and the same country, so that it was easy to go from one conference to the other. Life and Work met at Oxford in July of 1937; Faith and Order met at Edinburgh in August. There was just time for a little rest and refreshment between the two!

Life and Work had found that practice alone was not enough, that it had to be founded on faith. It had seen that a disinterested concern with faith possessed an extraordinarily practical value, because the example of the Confessing Church proved that a simple profession of faith in the Lordship of Jesus Christ was the most immediately effective thing that could be imagined. The two movements had come very close together. Their amalgamation was decided upon then, although it was not formally ratified until the following year, 1938. From that fusion, the World Council of Churches was to be born. But, just as the First World War had, if not stopped, at least slowed down and increased the difficulty of efforts toward reunion, so also, in 1939, the Second World War postponed the moment when decisions could be realized. The World Council of Churches remained, as they say, "in formation," and received its official constitution only through the agreement of the member Churches at Amsterdam, in August of 1948.

What exactly is the World Council of Churches? The word "council" is fitting in one way, but not in another. It is not fitting if it suggests a felt-covered table around which grave discussions are held, because the World Council is less a table for discussion than a world-wide platform for meetings. But the word *is* fitting if one thinks about the significance that now attaches to the Council of Europe. That Council enjoys no sovereignty; it cannot make any executive decisions through its member countries. It is simply a meeting-ground where attempts are made, through the work of technical commissions, to prepare the way very slowly for a united, or at least a federated, Europe. It is extremely difficult work, because everything varies from country to country, especially legislation. Recently, at

Strasbourg, a new bridge across the Rhine was to be built jointly by the French and the Germans. Nothing could seem easier at first glance than to have French and German engineers and workers collaborating over the construction of a bridge. In reality it turned out to be very complicated, because neither social laws, work standards, safety measures, or salaries were the same. This is only an example, but it shows that a very long time and innumerable discussions will be necessary to reduce the differences and arrive at a point where Europe could be federated and, perhaps, united.

The World Council of Churches has a certain analogy with the Council of Europe. It is a meeting place of Christian Churches or communions, each of which remains absolutely sovereign. It cannot in any way impose anything on anyone. Its members remain perfectly free. Each of them comes to meet other Churches, while retaining full sovereignty over its own doctrinal or ecclesiastical decisions. The Council offers them the opportunity for discussion among themselves, together with a number of services and organizations comparable to those existing in the Council of Europe. The Churches can thus compare their points of view, engage in joint studies, and make their way little by little toward a common Christian consciousness. Since New Delhi, when several new Churches were admitted (Moscow, Bulgaria, and Romania among them), the World Council has numbered 198 different Christian communions of varying importance. For instance, ten of the Methodist Churches of the United States form ten unities in the World Council, although there is only one Methodism; and similarly, various Lutheran Churches of the United States, springing from the diverse origins of immigrant groups (Baltic States, Germany, Scandinavia, Hungary, etc.), form as many different unities in the Council, although there is only one Lutheranism. In all, six major groups belong to the World Council: Lutherans, Calvinists, Methodists, Baptists, Anglicans, and the Orthodox Churches. Added to these, like satellites, are various smaller Churches which are completely autonomous and sovereign.

The complexity of the problems arising can easily be imagined. To summon a council within the Catholic Church is already hard enough. They are wondering in Rome how a deliberative assembly of 2,800 people is to be organized: what agenda to adopt, how to apportion the subjects, how much time to give to the speakers, etc. And yet the Catholic Church has a unity of doctrine, a unity of language (our poor ecclesiastical Latin), and a unity of structure. Compared with that, what must the difficulties be for the World Council, which includes so many different organizations, and so many different languages—and not only national languages like English, French, and German, but different theological languages too—an immense variety of categories belonging to over fifty countries. It was a gamble! But the gamble paid off. The undeniable fact is that it works, and works very well.

But those are only the exterior aspects. The World Council of Churches has another aspect which is infinitely more interesting. The first chapter of ecumenism, from 1910 to 1937, was characterized, as I have said, by lateral confessional conversations, by a dialogue going on in many different directions on one level. But the Confessing Church of Germany, by referring itself vertically, so to speak, to the Lord Jesus Christ, found that it had become one, and that it was capable of assuming the responsibility of giving a witness to the world. Now this is exactly what has happened in the course of the second chapter of ecumenism, that of the World Council. It has passed from the horizontal to the vertical plane, from a preoccupation with mutual questionings and a dialogue between confession and confession, to a fidelity to the one Gospel and a road of common obedience. It is this fidelity which enables the divided Churches to remain together, and faithfully to exercise their responsibility toward the world.

Often, at the end of his life, a man comes back to the things he loved and the places where he lived as a child. The same could be said of the World Council: it is returning to its origins, which were entirely conditioned by missionary work. It all began from the desire to present the pagan world with a single teaching, and to assume the fullest responsibility for preaching the Gospel to the heathen of every land. That was the slogan of the Young Men's Christian Associations of the nineteenth century, which was expressed by the President of the Federation in these terms: "The evangelization of the whole world by the present generation." That generation has passed away, but it has seen its work already partly achieved. The new generation will have to continue it. The great innovation in the World Council of Churches is that differences and oppositions are being left, as it were, in parentheses.

Formerly, the separated communions tried to harmonize their points of view, however slightly, by lateral conversations. Now, they are not trying to go that way. They forget the differences, or step over them somehow, and listen to the Lord's voice instead. They ask him what he wants of us at this moment; and he answers that what he wants now is for us to undertake the evangelization of the world—together. If we follow faithfully and obediently the Lord's call, it will be given us to perform this task of world evangelization, and at the same time to find unanimity.

It was in this spirit that a fusion took place at New Delhi between the World Council of Churches and quite a different organization, the World Council of Missions, which had been in existence since the beginning of the century. This was not easily done, because the two organizations had dissimilar structures and were not covering exactly the same ground. The World Council of Churches, as its name implies, includes only Churches. The World Council of Missions includes Churches certainly, but also the missionary societies which were formed by private initiative in the nineteenth century, of which we have already spoken. Furthermore, the Council of Missions is purely Protestant, whereas the Council of Churches includes a certain number of Orthodox Churches (the Church of

Greece, the Church of Egypt, and the Patriarchate of Constantinople). Since New Delhi, three more of the great Orthodox Churches, those of Russia, Romania, and Bulgaria, have also become members. The entry of these other Orthodox Churches and the fusion with the Council of Missions took place simultaneously. The two events, at least on the level of human reactions, undoubtedly favored each other's success. The Orthodox, who might have feared a more extreme "Protestantization" of the World Council, felt reassured by the advent of three great Churches. And at the same time, the integration of the Council of Missions and the World Council must have been reassuring to the Protestants, who had courageously and loyally accepted the fact of Orthodox numerical preponderance.

The integration of the Council of Missions, which has now been accomplished, was an essentially logical consequence of the ideas that have been inspiring the World Council since the end of the last war. This logic was well expressed at Evanston by A. Nygren, the author of *Eros and Agapè*: "We can say nothing valid about the Church if we speak of her without at the same time meaning Jesus Christ. This means that we must leave the periphery and go to the center, instead of cataloguing our different conceptions and noting the agreements or disagreements that result from them. We are being led to the very heart of the Christian faith; and the command we receive there is not to expound our own denominational points of view, but to be taught together by the Word of God.

Then we shall verify the truth that it is by going to the center that we find unity." In this same perspective the words of Karl Adam are often quoted in World Council circles: "Jesus Christ is the personality of the Church."

These words finely express the inspiration of this second chapter of the Ecumenical Movement. No longer is there lateral discussion leading to a reduction of differences; instead, there is a *search*, undertaken together in a single responsibility toward the world and in vertical obedience to the same Lord and the same Gospel—and all are finding themselves unified in this obedience. We have, as Catholics, an effort to make if we are to penetrate completely into this perspective, because we think of the unity of the Church as an already existing framework into which it is simply a matter of entering.

The fine and ample text of the First Vatican Council (1869-1870) on the Church contains a dogmatic constitution entitled "First Dogmatic Constitution on the Church" (it therefore calls for a second, which it will be the task of Vatican II to elaborate), and it begins with the words *Pastor aeternus,* the "Eternal Pastor." How does this constitution envisage the Church? It sees the Church as a completed house into which you must go if you are not in it, in which you must stay if you are in it, remaining there under the conduct of those who are invested with authority. These authorities are named very rapidly, in order finally to pass (because this is what it has been leading up to) to the sole and supreme Pastor, the pope. And after that, it is mainly concerned with the pope. Hence the Church is presented by this document in a static way, essentially as a frame or as a home. This is true of course; a biblical phrase calls it "the House of God." But there is not even a mention of the laymen who live in it and who are under submission to the pastors. This static view has repercussions throughout the whole Church, right down to the conception of the parish. This again is thought of as already built, not only with regard to its material buildings, but in relation to its work, its organizations, into which one is simply required to enter and remain under the conduct of a pastor. This is a static and very clerical conception! It will seem too formal to our Protestant brothers of the Ecumenical Movement, and rather empty, although it certainly contains quite a bit of truth.

At the end of a lecture in which I had made these remarks, the wife of a Protestant pastor said to me, "Father, you are right; but all the same there's a lot of truth in the conception of the parish as you described it. It's something we rather lack, this solid frame into which one ought to go, and stay in, if one is in it already." However, I still believe that this conception seems rather too formal to our Protestant brothers.

In any case, the Ecumenical Movement has a much more dynamic conception of the Church: her unity is not so much given, as it is to be created. Yet, on this point, the Protestants need to understand that it is not *only* a reality which remains *to be created*. The Church, according to them, is certainly a gift of God, but she does not receive her unity unless she is faithful, and therefore exercising her responsibility toward the world. Here, unquestionably, there is a deficiency, a lack: unity, in the Protestant mind, is more of the order of events than of the institution, if I may quote the categories that have been so happily revived by Pastor J.-L. Leuba. For my part, I think that both conceptions contain a great deal of truth. The Catholic conception of the Church is that she was founded by Jesus Christ and the Apostles in a stable and real way; in the end, the Protestants will have to recognize this. There are prerequisites for her mission—apostolicity and tradition among them—because the Gospel has a content which needs to be explained. But there is also an extremely profound truth in the missionary ideology with which, in the second chapter of its history, the Ecumenical Movement has been identified. Institution and mission are in no way contradictory. The Church cannot be fully the Church of Jesus Christ unless she is the intermediary and messenger of Jesus Christ for the world.

In this connection it is interesting to follow the evolution of the themes discussed at the major conferences of the World Council. At Amsterdam, in 1948, it was "Man's Disorder and God's Plan"; at Evanston, in 1954, it was "Jesus Christ, the Hope of the World"; and at New Delhi, in 1961, "Jesus Christ, the Light of the World." In these three themes there is a common structure: one pole which is God or Jesus Christ; and one pole which is the world. The pole of God or Jesus

Christ is a plan, or a hope, or a light. The world-pole is a disorder, or a lack of hope, or darkness that needs to be enlightened. In fact, the Ecumenical Movement conceives itself as a quest for unity. It situates this unity in the dynamic and living conjunction between the two terms: the bringing of God's plan into the world's disorder; the bringing of Christ's hope into the foolish world of men; the bringing of Christ's light into a world in darkness.

Not only are the themes of these great world assemblies significant, but also the places where they met. We are going to hold a Council at Rome. Would this Council happen in the same way if it were meeting at Dakar, or in India, or in South America? Probably not. Places have their value. The Church of Rome, with the prestige and the grandeur that the centuries have given her, officially imposes a certain orientation on the Council. It would not be the same thing if it were meeting at Oxford, or New York, or Buenos Aires. But the World Council meets at one time in Holland, the next time in the United States, and last time in India, because it has a world structure. This world structure is not possessed by the Catholic Church in the same way: hers is centralized (one could compare it to a pyramid whose base converges toward its summit); that of the World Council is more dispersed and, in this respect, more world-wide. Its most influential members, its Presidents and Secretary General, are constantly traveling about the world. They have direct personal contacts in every country with the men who are immediately confronted with the problems. They are not made to come to the Roman scene, which is charming no doubt, but a little too much removed from actuality. Finding ourselves in St. Peter's Square, we wonder if we are still under the pontificate of Pius V! Truth is syntheses and fullness: we must join the dynamic conception to the static conception of the Church; the idea of a given Church to that of a Church in the making; the reality of a Church bound up with a center that gives her an axis of certitude, to that of a Church more widely dispersed about the world.

We are certainly very far into the second chapter of the World Council of Churches. Probably there will be a third before the end of the book. God alone knows when and how it will be written. Shall we be writing it with our separated brothers, or will they continue to write it without us? No one can say. At the present moment there is nothing to prevent us from going on, as we have in the past, with the work we have undertaken alongside our Protestant and Orthodox brothers. Although we do not take part officially in the World Council of Churches, we are participating in very real ways in its efforts—and not only through prayer, which is the bearer of true spiritual forces, but also in theological work, through human encounters, documentation, and dialogue. Would it be possible to go further? Could a new chapter open in which we were active partners? I think that the time is not yet ripe, either on our side or on theirs, and perhaps even less on theirs than ours. The official entry of the

Catholic Church into the World Council of Churches would create almost insoluble problems, or, in any case, extremely difficult ones. It could have dangerous consequences for the World Council itself, composed as it is of a majority of Protestants for whom a massive Catholic invasion would bring terrible difficulties, psychological, intellectual, and human. On our side too, although maturation has been making progress from year to year, it is not finished yet. However, certain events are accelerating it. The new climate of John XXIII's pontificate, the proximity of the Council, and the creation of the Secretariat for Christian Unity are unmistakable signs of a profound transformation. The Secretariat for Unity has shown itself to be very open, and is already playing a considerable role. Is it not significant that the Anglican Church should have a permanent delegate accredited to a Catholic Secretariat? It is the first time in history that such an event has happened. This is only a sign perhaps, but it is an eloquent one, and we may salute it as the dawn of hope.

4

The Council and the Need for Dialogue

The first part of this essay will give the reasons why a Christian who wishes to be adult today must be a man of dialogue. The second and shorter part will apply these ideas to the Council, suggesting what it might be, or at least what we all hope it may be.

First of all, the Christian who desires to have an adult faith today must be a man who is open to dialogue. I say today, to describe one of the spiritual situations in our present world in contrast to what it was before the sixteenth century. The sixteenth century was both the time of the birth of the modern world and of the outbreak and establishment of the Reformation. Undoubtedly the "Reformation" cannot be equated with "the modern world," but the events were contemporaneous, almost twins, and they have indisputable similarities of spirit and attitude. We must see, then, what the situation was before the sixteenth century and what it has since become. I shall proceed by successive approaches.

The Present Necessity for Dialogue

FIRST APPROACH

Before the sixteenth century, that is, from the time of the Church Fathers and all through the Middle Ages, from about the fourth to the sixteenth centuries, only one spiritual world existed in the West: that constituted by the Roman Catholic Church. The Church was really the sole spiritual world; she gave men their intellectual certainty, the framework of their thoughts, the direction of their lives. It was she who brought them the beauty that they needed, through her liturgy, her feasts, the beautiful poetry of her legends, her buildings, her cathedrals, her illuminated manuscripts, her singing. She provided men with an indispensable element in their lives: poetry and dreams; in a word, she was the holy Ark of culture. In the Middle Ages, when the word *clericus* was used, it meant "a man who knows how to read and write"; and often, instead of calling a layman *laicus,* he was described as *illiteratus,* a man who cannot read, or at least who cannot read Latin.

Naturally, men of that time knew of the existence of others who did not belong to the Church; these others lived beyond, outside the frontiers of Christianity. In the Middle Ages people often spoke of the *Aethiops,* the Black, the Ethiopian. They knew about Africa; they knew that on the far side of Persia lay the Indies, and beyond the Indies other countries. St. Louis sent an embassy of Preaching Friars and Minors to the Great Kahn of Mongolia, and we have their story. Hence there was awareness of the existence of other communities beyond the fringes of Christianity, living in a different spiritual world from that of the Church. But, if their existence was known, it was represented in an extremely legendary fashion. This can be seen in the carvings on the tympanum at Vézelay, where the un-evangelized heathen have been given the heads of dogs. And not only was their representation legendary; there was very little concern about them. It is striking to see the lack of curiosity in the men of the Middle Ages about what was beyond their knowledge. Nowadays, we have an exactly contrary mentality, that of not being able to bear the sight of a barrier without wanting to go straight through it! Joinville tells, in his delightful account of the expedition of St. Louis to Egypt, how every morning they found exotic fruits floating on the muddy waters of the Nile. Whether they were pine-apples or mandarins is of small importance. "It is said," he adds, "that these fruits come from the terrestrial paradise, and that if we went sufficiently far up the Nile we should find it." It was enough for him to report the observation; I agree that he did not have the leisure to go and see, but I think he also lacked the desire.

The men of the Middle Ages were very incurious, then, very unconcerned about others. In Western Christianity also there were "others"—the Jews, for example, and, from the end of the eleventh century on, the spiritual sects, among them the Waldenses at the end of the twelfth and the beginning of the thirteenth centuries. The Jews were kept under strict control in their ghettos; the spiritual sects, if they made themselves too manifest, were silenced, by force if necessary. The occasions of contact with the Holy Bible were rare at a time when the smallest manuscript of the Holy Book cost the price of one or two horses. But the faithful continually heard the Bible spoken of in sermons; they saw it in the stained glass windows and sculptures of the cathedrals; they heard its words in stories which were embroidered with legends. On the dogmatic level, independently of the detail of the creeds—where there were certainly some differences of interpretation—there was only one way of reading the Bible, the basis of Christian doctrine, and that was the way of the Church. In the sixteenth century everything changed; in the West the Bible becomes a book that both unites and divides us, as soon as one begins to read and explain it.

In those days, then, there was a single spiritual world. By contrast, the modern universe is characterized by the existence of several spiritual worlds, and even more by the existence of several Christian spiritual worlds.

Since the sixteenth century there has been a complete break between the Christian East and West. The rift had been growing for centuries, because there never was a community of feeling between the East and West. Anyone who travels in the Near East and mixes with the Orthodox (Eastern Christians who are not united to the See of Rome) notices that everything is both extremely similar between them and us, and **extremely** different. There are the same sacraments, the same priesthood, the same monastic life, the same worship of the Virgin Mary, the same Trinitarian and Christological doctrines—in spite of the different formulation of the doctrine on the Holy Spirit. We hold all of these things, fundamentally, in common, and yet everything is different. They celebrate the Eucharist otherwise; they live the religious life otherwise; they feel things differently; their intellectual construction of Christian truths is different. In a word, it is another spiritual world, but one which exercises its mysterious influence over us.

In the sixteenth century, in the West, the Reformation was born. It introduced yet another spiritual world. It is impossible not to be struck by the following fact: while the Church Fathers or the ancient Councils found themselves faced with divergences or heresies bearing on one particular chapter of Christian doctrine—the Holy Trinity, predestination, or the Eucharist—the great modern dissidences are divisions in the Christian consciousness itself. The Christian consciousness is divided between two or several differing interpretations, each of which claims to be the whole Christianity; we are invited to establish with God, in Jesus Christ, a new kind of religious relationship.

But there exist other spiritual worlds, different from that of the Catholic Church: the non-Christian spiritual worlds. I call a spiritual world an aggregation of ideas and values capable of nourishing a man's consciousness and of giving a meaning to his own destiny and to the destiny of others. These worlds have names: Judaism, Islam, Buddhism. There even exists a lay spiritual world, in the French sense of the word "lay." The word does not simply mean "one who is neither cleric nor monk," but designates someone who has freed himself from the positive dogmas of a Church and the influence of a clergy. We have laymen of this kind in France. Although some of them possess negative outlooks, there are many who cherish and who have dedicated their consciences to moral and even spiritual values, such as fraternity, humanity, progress, science, reason, peace —and other values equivalent to these that are very respectable, and have names that are often written with capital letters. They represent absolutes, and for many men are an alibi or a hiding place for God.

There exists too a proletarian spiritual world, which is not materialist, and which entertains an aggregation of ideas and values that are capable of nourishing a man's consciousness and of giving a final meaning to his own destiny and that of others. This proletarian spiritual world has been a heady discovery, since the last war, for many Christian young people, mainly from the bourgeoisie, for a number of clergy, and for a great many intellectuals. They have discovered a world where fraternity, or peace, are objects of a truly mystical love, a world which easily moves men to share and carry the burdens of others along with their own.

All of these worlds are characterized more exactly by two traits. First, they are, or believe themselves to be, or claim to be, *complete*. It is very true that, for us, where God is lacking, there is only a terrible emptiness. But they do not feel that way; or else, more probably, they have replaced God by something else and have given him another name. Under words like "peace," and "progress," and "fraternity," often there exists the worship of an unknown God. These are complete worlds. I am thinking, for example, of a book by Roger Vaillant, *Un jeune homme seul,* where he describes the death and civil burial of a communist worker. Over the still-open grave, different people say quite simply that the man was a good husband, a good father, a good trade union member; he went to night school, he studied, he helped others out of their ignorance. While these words are being spoken, they outline the life of a man who, knowing nothing of God, was still not a material-ist. A certain number of values constituted his spiritual world; these values were erroneous ones, no doubt, but his world was complete and coherent. It is important for us to realize this if we want to understand the world around us.

The second characteristic of such spiritual worlds is that they are *the object of an experience.* They can be completely entered only by conversion, by a passage from one state to another, which is the essence of con-version and is like a new birth. Those who have had the experience of freedom, of prayer, of the presence of God, or of the power of Scripture know that they have had an irreplaceable experience, one that cannot be communicated by words or ideas to anyone who has not had it. In his book, *De la vraie et de la fausse con-*

version, Léon Brunschvicg describes false conversion as conversion to mysticism: it leads to an impasse and an alibi. True conversion is the conversion to science, to mathematical reason, which gives the key to reality. At least he was speaking in terms of conversion, and that is the significant thing.

SECOND APPROACH

In the guise of an introduction to the second approach, it would be appropriate to read a most savory text from Sire de Joinville's *History of Saint Louis.* The passage could be entitled, "An Ecumenical Conference in the Thirteenth Century."

He (King St. Louis) told me that there was a great conference of clerics and Jews at the monastery of Cluny. There was a knight there to whom the Abbot had given bread for the love of God, and he asked the Abbot to allow him to say the first word, which they granted him reluctantly. And then he got up and leant on his crutch and said that they should bring in the greatest of the clerics and the greatest Rabbi of the Jews. And thus it was done. And the knight put to the Rabbi a question, which was this: "Master," he said to him, "I ask you if you believe that the Virgin Mary who bore God in her womb and in her arms, gave birth as a virgin, and that she is the mother of God?" And the Jew replied that of all that he believed nothing. And the knight answered him that he had truly acted like a fool when, neither believing in her nor loving her, he had entered her church and her house; and, said the knight, you shall pay me for it. And then he lifted his crutch and struck the Jew behind the ear and threw him to the ground. And the Jews took flight, carrying away their wounded

Rabbi, and so ended the conference. "And this I say to you," said the King, "that no one, unless he is a very good clerk, should argue with them. But a layman, when he hears evil spoken of the Christian faith, should not defend the Christian faith unless with the sword, and this he should give them in the belly as far as it will go."

I wanted to give this text for two reasons. The first reason, on which I shall not dwell, is that it makes one think about what may be called the Christian roots of anti-Semitism. Many of us have read *The Last of the Just* by André Schwarz-Bart. This is certainly a rather simplistic book and very unfair to Christians; but it is powerful and capable of making us think, as we read, about Christian responsibility, with the caution, however, that medieval anti-Semitism was never on a racial basis, but on the basis of faith against misbelief. Of course this did not prevent it from being just about as violent.

But the question I want to ask you primarily is, what kind of a picture existed in the mind of this good crutch-wielding knight of Cluny? He saw the truth as something complete, proclaimed once and for all, rigorously identical with the dogmas preached by the Catholic Church, outside which there could be only error, nothingness, and vanity. Did it ever occur to him to wonder whether the Jew had had the possibility, the chance, the means of knowing the Christian faith, and whether it was his duty to know it? Or what might have been the conscious motives of this man, or his personal experiences? No, he simply considered the truth in itself; and, if he did not find it as it should be, he acted in the accepted way of the time—scandalous to us—by using force.

Look how different our feelings are today. Here is an example, or a personal impression. During a Unity Week in Poitou, I noted in passing the text of a Memento for the Living and a Memento for the Dead, which read: "Let us all pray for our separated brethren who lived as Christians and died in fidelity to their faith." The text comes from a spiritual universe totally different from that of the knight of Cluny, and one which would have made no sense to him. Speaking of fidelity to "their" faith? For him there was only one faith, the objective, the true faith, that of the Church. He did not consider the faith of a dedicated conscience, to which there might also be loyalty and fidelity.

A little before the last war, in 1939, I was received in audience by Cardinal Baudrillart, who had known me as a young student at the Catholic Institute of Paris and who was very fond of me. He was a man who was outspoken to the point of brutality. "How is it," he asked me, "that you Preaching Friars have got there ('there' meaning to the level of tolerance), you, the sons of the Inquisition?" I said to him, "Eminence, I have got 'there' through exactly the same love of truth for which my brothers of those days created the Inquisition."

But this love of truth is applied to two different worlds, and in two absolutely opposite ways: in a world of truth-in-itself, love of truth can lead to the Inquisition; in a world where account is taken of the strivings of men and their quest for the true, love of truth leads to a respect for every element of the true, even when it is mixed with error, so that, in rejecting the one, the other is not lost. One hundred and fifty years from now it will seem astonishing that we could have tolerated certain abuses around us in the order of social structures, colonialism, or the cold war in which we are living. We are swallowing up hundreds of millions, instead of building houses and hospitals! These social structures, which are the reflections of our ideas, have brought us to the point where we are. In the name of social truth we must be tolerant, not out of weakness of intelligence, nor out of softness, nor out of false liberalism—but out of love of truth. No one possesses the whole of truth; thus we cannot totally respect truth unless we respect it also in those in whom it is mixed with errors. Our effort must be to free it from these errors and to reincorporate it in a body of truth. But it is absolutely impossible for that to be done immediately.

I join myself unreservedly to the formula that was expressed a few years ago by Walter Dirks. He called tolerance *Leidenschaft für die Wahrheit,* passion for the truth. For every element of truth which is at present perhaps mixed with errors, I have the same respect that I should feel for a wafer of the Host that had fallen to the ground.

THIRD APPROACH

In quite a number of countries today every one can be sure of working with or living on the same street with, sometimes even in the same apartment building, a Protestant neighbor, a Jew, perhaps a communist, and four or five more who are indifferent. Compose your palette as you like, it is certain to be extremely varied. We cannot live in a purely homogeneous world at the present time. This is of the greatest importance because there is one question nowadays that is always coming up: "The others? How about the others?" Recently, at Friburg in Brisgau, the French chaplain invited me to say a few words to his senior high school boys and girls who were sixteen or seventeen years old. All of these young people asked me questions that *we* were hardly raising at the age of twenty-five, serious questions which showed a certain level of religious knowledge. And their questions all came back to this: "What about the others? Why is it that I believe and they don't? And if they aren't believers, will they be saved? And another thing—these are my close friends, and they can easily find out about Christian truth. But what about the others? The Chinese, for instance? In our world of today, one man in four is a Chinaman. What chance have they of knowing about Jesus Christ? None, or almost none. So then, what happens to them?" At the end of the school year, I gave two lectures to the Catholic students of Strasbourg on ecumenism. One student got up and asked me in a very deep voice: "Father, would you please tell me what is

the place of the Reformation in God's plan?" This is
a very difficult question; but note the way in which
it was put. Sixty years ago, a student would certainly
not have put that question in those terms. Those terms
implied that, beyond the canonical or dogmatic con-
demnation, which was not mentioned, there remained
a problem, stated in reference to a criterion that escapes
us. I had to admit that I knew nothing about it and
could offer no judgment, but that God knew.

At the end of these three successive approaches, it
only remains to tie up the package and to interpret the
results. Today, a Catholic who is fully conscious can
no longer think that Christianity exists uniquely within
the Church; and the Church herself can no longer
think out her problems simply within her own frame
of reference. Naturally the Church will always see
them in terms of her own tradition, in which Holy
Scripture is the supreme element. Do not expect her
to formulate her social doctrine on the basis of the principles of Marxism, or to reconsider her Christian doctrine starting from the principles of the Reformation.
The Church can think of her problems only on the
basis of her own principles of existence, of her own
tradition, of the treasure that God has confided to her
and that she has the mission to carry across the centuries.
But it is possible to imagine that she might try,
while thinking of her problems, to include in her thinking the relations of others with her, and her own relations with others. A few years ago, Father J. Levie,

S.J., wrote a book called *Sous les yeux de l'incroyant.* The book well illustrated its title, because its theme was that a Christian, a Catholic, must nowadays act, think, behave, as though he were under the eyes of an unbeliever, being watched by him and, as it were, mutely interrogated. We have to include now in our behavior the thought of the existence of the others, the questions that the others will ask us, either silently or aloud. The Church will always find the answers in her own tradition, but they will no longer apply simply to her problems, conceived exclusively within an internal frame of reference; they will be answers to problems posed by her existence mixed with that of others, the existence of others around her and in the midst of her. And this is a source of immense riches. When we conduct a monologue with ourselves, we run the risk of becoming impoverished and enclosed in the narrow circle of our own thoughts. That can be comfortable, like a habit that keeps us warm, but we can finally rediscover ourselves only by facing ourselves. Furthermore, the dialogue will force answers from us that we were carrying implicitly, but that we should never have expressed if we had not been obliged to speak in some way.

I shall set down for you at this point—for want of a text of St. Augustine's in which he said the same thing at the beginning of the fifth century—a passage from Paul Claudel's speech on the occasion of his reception into the Académie Française. Claudel described first of all the setting of his childhood and youth, the 1890's,

the Dreyfus affair, and the very virulent anticlericalism
of that time. He was an unbeliever himself then, and
his friends were unbelievers as well, particularly the
two whom he mentioned in his speech and remembered
with the tenderest friendship. These were the Berthe-
lots, the chemist and the statesman, and both were most
ardent anticlericalists. Claudel said:

> This complex of movements, the Dreyfus affair, the
> protests that it raised, its backwash, had nevertheless two
> characteristics in common; these were its spontaneity,
> and then above all that it happened outside the Church,
> and was in fact in contradiction and in some respects in
> violent opposition to her. But, in the words that St.
> Paul puts into the mouth of our Mother: "Who can ask
> a question without my being questioned?" It is not only
> to those who are her new friends without knowing it—
> and who are coming in from all the corners of the earth
> to her who was called deserted—it is to her enemies that
> the Church of God says: I was waiting for you, here I
> am, and all that I have to say to you is, "Blessed is he
> that comes to me in the name of the Lord." If you strike
> me, it is because you have need of me. Knock, and it
> shall be opened to you; knock, and you will not be dis-
> appointed. It is enough if all these questions, under all
> their shapes and forms, the most insidious or the most
> brutal, can draw out of me that which was in me and
> belonged to you, that part of the Word of God which
> was hidden away in me and was intended for you, that
> word in me which was appropriate to each one of you
> and was indispensable to you.

To put it a little differently, other people's questions
compel us to release from ourselves an answering spark.
The spark would otherwise have remained buried in

us, and we should not have produced the answer that was occasioned by the shock of the question.

So it is that the Catholic Church is open to dialogue. Without being a member of the World Council of Churches—it is not certain that our Protestant brothers would wish it—she has other means at her disposal for entering into dialogue with them. These means are based on a whole scale of activities that moves from the tolerated up to the quasi-official, by way of the permitted and the helpful. The scale has a great number of tones: the Catholic Church possesses an extremely refined canonical, legal, and diplomatic tradition; she has, perhaps more than most, a considerable variety of resources in this domain with which it is important to be well acquainted, from friendship and fraternization on the human level up to doctrinal and theological dialogue.

But one cannot reach any depth, even along theological lines, unless one fulfills the necessary spiritual conditions, the first of which is prayer. Prayer has always one infallible result, that of changing our hearts, even if we do not always receive what we ask for, and especially in the way in which we were expecting it. When we have prayed together and have started a dialogue, a level of exchange is reached where that which was formerly impossible, and would still be so today—to take it simply on the level of discussion—will become possible tomorrow. Certainly we have not yet reached substantial agreements, officially recognized on both sides; but some of the road has been covered.

There are agreements that are working on the helpful and personal levels in a remarkable way.

The Council and Ecumenical Dialogue

This second and shorter part, in the form of a conclusion, will apply to the future Council some ideas which I hope I have established and explained. Two years ago, when Pope John XXIII declared his intention of calling an ecumenical council, the mere announcement immediately raised immense hopes throughout the world. The Secretary-General of the United Nations wrote that the Council, with its infinite possibilities, would be the greatest event of the century, and possibly, he added, of several centuries. On certain conditions, naturally, this would be true. Charles Malik is a Lebanese Orthodox and he was thinking of the possibilities of a closer union between East and West, an immense step toward the reconciliation of Christians, and toward world peace.

There was a slight misunderstanding at first about the Holy Father's announcement. Since he had used the word "invitation," it was believed that the other Churches would be invited, particularly as John XXIII had made his speech on January 25, the closing day of the Week of Universal Prayer for Unity. This was an ecumenical context, intentionally chosen, which immediately gave his proposal a strong air of union. Again, many people were misled by the word "ecumenical," for they took it in the sense that the newspapers have often given it during these last twenty years in speaking of the Ecumenical Movement or the World Council of Churches. But ecumenical is a word that means simply world-wide; in English, the official title of the ecumenical council of the Church is "World Council." The word "ecumenical" has been used since the fourth century in the Catholic Church to designate councils to which the whole of the Catholic episcopate, that is, the bishops united to the See of Rome, was invited. The explanations came later. To tell the truth, no one who knows his theology could ever have thought that, the Council being a Church affair, there could be any question of Protestant delegates taking part. It was not a conference; a council supposes ecclesiastical communion: unity in the faith, in the Eucharistic celebration, in the recognition of apostolic authority.

It may be objected that the Council, being an internal affair of the Catholic Church, will simply deal with the Church's internal problems, principally the pastoral and missionary ones. In any case the pope had declared that it would proceed to a wise modernization of the Church and her adaptation to present-day needs. However, there was more than this in the official text of January 25, 1959: "The Council has not simply for its aim, in the thought of the Holy Father, the spiritual welfare of Christian people, but is intended equally to be an invitation to the separated communities to seek the unity to which so many souls are aspiring today in all parts of the earth." After that, there were many declarations, either by the Pope—for example, that of August 9, 1959—or by qualified members of the cardinalate. Cardinal Tisserant declared on August 25 of the same year: "The Council is an internal affair of the Catholic Church, but it would wish nevertheless to work usefully in the direction of unity, so that after the Council we shall be able to approach the problems of unity in a new and more favorable manner."

These official declarations go very far, since they affirm that the Council has for its ulterior and distant aim the service of Christian unity—a "unionic tele-finality." This is of extreme importance: the Council must itself, from the moment of its preparation, which began on Easter of 1959, until the time when it is held, have its outlook oriented toward the "others." Hence there will be a certain amount of dialogue, in one way or another. This does not imply that Protestant delegates will have the right to speak—although such a possibility is not ruled out—but, to quote Father Levie's expression again, the Council will be held, not under the eyes of unbelievers, but under the eyes of all our separated brethren. We must act as if they had their attention fixed on us; as if, silently or aloud, they were questioning us and hoping for something from us.

In concrete terms, what will happen? We can try to conjecture it without entering the field of theological fiction or unhampered imagination, but remaining within the limits of the possible and the reasonable, and even of the formally anticipated and announced. We could first envisage that, in the preparatory work, at least on certain subjects, account would be taken of the positions of others, Protestants, Orthodox, Anglicans, whether Catholic theologians are asked for reports about the positions of these others in regard to such or such points, or whether they themselves are asked—and this would probably be even better. In any case, we shall do our best to make it happen like this; and, if Christian people want it, perhaps they will be heard—this might be of considerable interest. First of all, from the dogmatic point of view, it would be very important to have a certain number of matters officially re-explained, so that we could explain them better ourselves as a result of what had been made clear to us. For, although the Council cannot change any of the Catholic dogmas, it can explain them better, and in such formulas or perspectives that various objections of our separated brethren would be met. I am thinking, for example, of points like the too famous *Ex sese, non autem ex consensu Ecclesiae* of the First Vatican Council: dogmatic decisions pronounced by the pope *ex cathedra* prevail by the authority of the pope, without the need of being validated by an act of the Church declaring them to be received. This is a point of doctrine about whose meaning the Orthodox continue to be confused. Could not the real sense be officially declared? Such an explanation would be beneficial. We have already tried it in private conversations; why should not these be generalized on the level of the Church?

In the missionary domain, the problems are often the same, either because of the ultrarapid industrialization of some formerly underdeveloped countries, or, more terrible still, because of the birth and frenzied development of political and cultural nationalism in a great number of countries. The problems these have raised exist for Protestant missions just as for Catholic ones, and very much in the same forms, even though neither side has the same doctrinal structure. Would it not be profitable to pool experiences, to know what methods have been tried out here or there? And would not the very fact of taking account of others in this way have a great value on its own?

But, during the Council itself, why could we not consider qualified theologians, Orthodox, Protestants, and Anglicans, coming to Rome and being accessible to furnish details of one sort or another, or so that they could be asked for reports on specific points? They could establish personal contacts, which are so beneficial and truly irreplaceable, and could inform their own communities of the progress of the Council's work, of the orientations of Catholic thought, of the advances that might be made to them, and of the opportunities that might present themselves. Did not the Pope himself declare, in an audience of August 30, 1959, that, if a number of the separated brethren wanted to be present at the Council, they would be received within reason? The words may not say much, but they have been explained since. Cardinal Tardini, at that time the Secretary of State charged with the preparation of the Council, held a two-and-one-half hour press conference on October 31 of the same year, during which he answered all the journalists' questions. He was asked whether Orthodox and Protestant theologians might be present at the Council. "The Council is an interior act of the Catholic Church," the Cardinal replied, "but it is probable that anyone who desires could be present as an observer. All will be gladly welcomed; and it seems that, in order for them to be able to follow the work, they will receive copies of the more important preparatory documents." Is this not what we might call a "green light"?

I say that a door is at least ajar, and I hope that those who could give it an extra push will be willing to open it completely, even if there is no possibility of a grand entry with a red carpet, an usher, and an organ, like those found at big weddings. We do not need that, anyway. If the door is ajar, then I beg them to be flexible and to do their bit. If no one does his bit, nothing will happen. And that would be worse than anything, because the Council has raised great hopes, and nothing is worse than disappointed hopes. Certainly not everything that we desire will be realized; this is why I am raising my sights a little. If only fifteen per cent of what I hope for gets through, that fifteen per cent will still represent something substantial.

I invite you to do the same. Catholic laymen can contribute greatly to the Council. First, they can contribute by fervent, daily prayer, because the devil always opposes everything big. And without any doubt he will oppose this as much as he can, on every rung of the ladder, from top to bottom. We are concerned with the Kingdom of God, with a spiritual work, with the history of salvation, with an event in the line of Pentecost. And the Apostles prayed that they might receive the Holy Spirit. Then, there is the effect that laymen can have on public opinion, because even in the Catholic Church public opinion does have an influence, a more powerful one than you might imagine. If the whole body of Christian people really shows a desire, and talks about it in a certain way, it will undoubtedly, at least in part, be granted. It must be done respectfully, avoiding any impatient demands for fulfillment, which have never been acceptable in the Church, but with frankness, as befits a Christian. This Council, more than any other perhaps, needs the initiative of laymen, because the Church is turning a corner in history. It needs prayer and the action of the Holy Spirit, who must be invoked without ceasing— the creative Spirit who can bring light into darkness, and where there was distrust, spread love.

5

1961—An Ecumenical Year

Starting from some very ordinarily observed facts, I should like to put to you a number of reflections. They will certainly not amount to a literary description, but will rather be a sort of analysis of the spiritual components of this quite remarkable ecumenical conjuncture that we are living through at the beginning of the year 1961.

The Ecumenical Conjuncture

To begin with, let us remind ourselves of some matters of common knowledge:

1. In the first place, during the past year, *various journeys have been undertaken by Church leaders*. The Patriarch of Constantinople visited the Patriarchates of Alexandria, Jerusalem, and Antioch; and recently the Patriarch Alexis of Moscow himself has been traveling through the Near East and in Greece. Patriarch Athenagoras of Constantinople has reiterated, to his visitors and to journalists, declarations that have become impressive by force of repetition, similar to the ones which he made to me personally in 1954: "If the

Pope leads the way, I will follow." For his part, Patriarch Alexis of Moscow declared at Athens: "If there were any question of opening negotiations with Rome, I should not need anyone's help. I could undertake them alone." This was perhaps a little like saying to Constantinople, "Please don't get mixed up in our affairs," but at least there was an allusion to Rome!

More recently still, there has been the Vatican visit of the Archbishop of Canterbury, the Most Rev. Geoffrey Francis Fisher. Although it does not appear to have been very extensive in scope, this meeting was extremely important. As has been said, it was a man to man contact, Churchman to Churchman, and better still, Christian to Christian. The simple fact that the visit took place was remarkable enough. On the Roman side, it created a delicate problem, since Leo XIII had declared against recognition of the Anglican Churches. How would the Archbishop be received? And how would he be addressed? "Your Grace"? Yes, the Pope called him "Your Grace." In taking the initiative himself, Dr. Fisher was courageously renewing a tie with Rome after four hundred years of separation. Without making any avowal, he was nonetheless recognizing the importance of the Roman See. It was a gesture of courage, because the Archbishop had on the one hand to resist the pressure of the Romanizing Anglo-Catholics behind him in England, who were happily remembering that Rome, by sending St. Augustine to Canterbury, had evangelized the island; and on the other hand he had to face the reactions of the Protestant side (the Scottish Presbyterians, for example, and others as well), who simply felt that he had gone too far.

In my opinion, this "courtesy visit" had a fairly precise object all the same: to unfreeze relations between Catholics and Anglicans in England itself, where these relations had become absolutely congealed! You may remember, for example, that when Rome published a document in December, 1949, officially authorizing Catholics to recite either the Lord's Prayer, or any other prayer approved by the Church, with their separated brethren, many of the English bishops refused to promulgate the document, since they would not agree to Catholics and Anglicans saying the Lord's Prayer together. Now, when an Anglican asks a Catholic to meet him, he will be able to say, "Don't be more papist than the pope!" Furthermore the Archbishop of Canterbury's visit to Rome was accompanied by equally significant moves in England. On the day of Dr. Fisher's reception at the Vatican, the Catholic Archbishop of Liverpool made a similar gesture in his own locality, inviting the Anglican Bishop of Liverpool to lunch. Several weeks previously, he had asked all his priests to do the same in their own parishes, with the corresponding Anglican clergy.

It was a small thing in one way, but very great in another; the situation was thawing.

It is apparent that, in these various moves (all of which I cannot mention), the Church leaders are not being pushed exactly, but at any rate they are being carried forward by their people, and they seem to be very much aware of this. They are taking initiatives that perhaps seem courageous to them, but, in reality, they are acting in response to a movement from below. I think that Pope John XXIII himself must have the feeling of being carried forward by a movement from below of Catholic opinion, which acts in a much more real way than is sometimes imagined, for, although it has no place in the official structure of the Church, it exercises a definite influence over her daily life.

2. Secondly, 1961 will be *an ecumenical year* because two great ecumenical events are in preparation or will take place this year.

First, the World Council of Churches will hold, at the end of November, its third world conference at New Delhi, India, on the theme of *Christ, the Light of the World*. This third conference will be an extremely important event. Not because the real work of a movement is done at these big assemblies, but because it may bring about a general shake-up in all of the Christian communions, thus helping the ecumenical idea along. (This will happen first, of course, among the members of the World Council, but also among ourselves, because of the actuality of the theme and the extensive press coverage that it will receive.) Ecumenism does in fact work a great deal through "shake-ups," not, for example, in the bad sense of shaking someone's legitimate convictions, but in the good sense in which it implies an inrush of vitality into a deathlike repose —another of the forward pushes of life.

The second great ecumenical event in preparation is the Council. Naturally the Council will not be opened this year (1961). Such monumental gatherings, involving thousands of people, require most careful preparation. Documents have to be circulated, and there are comings and goings and meetings which always take up a lot of time. In any case, however, the idea of the Council has powerfully seized the imagination of Catholics. Christians everywhere are interested in it. A number of excellent journalists are doing their best to keep this interest alive, and to maintain the Christian world in a state of optimism and expectancy.

Although these two ecumenisms can hardly be said to coincide—the problems arise precisely from the fact that they are beginning to meet—they are not unrelated. As you know, the Holy Father has said that the Council is to be primarily an internal affair of the Catholic Church, a bringing up to date, a "wise modernization"; but, from the beginning, he has laid down as its "tele-finality" that it should work effectively in the direction of reunion. On November 14, 1960, when the phase of preparatory work was solemnly inaugurated at St. Peter's, the Pope gave a speech in which he alluded to a very real difficulty. A Secretariat had been created, principally to inform the Protestants, Orthodox, and Anglicans about the preparatory work for the Council and the work of the Council itself. But the difficulty which immediately arose was that the preparatory work had to be secret. Rome likes to work seriously; displaying things in public simply invites discussions, in-

terpretations, misunderstandings, and prevents one from
working in peace. So the work had to be carried out
in secret, as it normally is. But then, how would the
Secretariat inform other people about work which is
secret by definition? This was the point the Holy Father
mentioned in his speech: "It is our hope that those
who, although not wholly professing the Catholic Faith,
honestly and truly desire to be informed of the work
of the Council, will not find it ill-timed or lacking in
courtesy if we invite them to wait until the members
of the various commissions have completed their work,
and all is ready and in order for those higher contacts
of intelligence, heart, and spiritual understanding, on
which may there rest the Spirit of the Lord." In this
fine, humble, and delicate text, the Pope seems to be
suggesting, perhaps in rather Sibylline fashion, that, between the preparation of the Council and the Council
itself, there will be a time for contacts with the "others."
Under what form? How can that be answered now?
There are things that experience alone can reveal.
Nevertheless the Pope's speech shows that he has not
absolutely abandoned his idea that the Council should
have as a long-term goal the preparation for contacts,
dialogue, and perhaps for closer relationships.

Obviously, if this is correct, that telefinality will
have to be kept in mind throughout the whole preparation of the Council. Here we see the great importance of the Secretariat for Christian Unity, which was
set up in June of 1960, at the same time as the Preparatory Commissions. The Pope put Cardinal Bea in

charge of this Secretariat, and the Cardinal chose Msgr. Willebrands as his secretary. That the latter is an authentic ecumenist has been as amply confirmed in Geneva as in Rome; no better choice could have been made. The Cardinal himself had directed the Biblical Institute at Rome for twenty years, and was for a long time confessor to Pope Pius XII; but the extent of his acquaintance with ecumenism was unknown, and I was waiting to see him at work with a curiosity that was mixed with the warmest interest at least, if not with suspense.

Last summer he held conferences and made statements in various countries, and I heard him speak in Italy at a meeting of Catholic ecumenists. As we came out, we said to each other, "This is a miracle! It is more than we could ever have hoped for." At this meeting, Cardinal Bea talked for forty minutes in French, and ended with words that were extraordinary enough coming from a cardinal. "And now," he said, "I should like to have your questions and criticisms." "Will your Secretariat," I asked him, "confine itself to informing non-Catholics about the Council and the preparations being made at Rome, or will it also undertake the opposite work of informing the Council about the thinking of the others?" "Most certainly it will," he replied, "and in fact I have already received a good number of reports, not only from Catholics but from Protestants, and I should like many more. Send them in; ask for them. Don't hesitate! My aim is to have the Council well and truly informed about Protestant, Anglican, and Orthodox thinking."

This seemed to me very important. To tell the truth, it will not be easy, because Commissions go back to a centuries-long tradition during the course of which no one has formed the habit of asking to be enlightened about the thinking of—shall we say—heretics. And that is what has to be done. Hence it is a difficult problem.

I have often asked myself, since the beginning of my ecumenical career—if I may be so bold as to call it that —whether I had the right to adopt a fundamentally different attitude toward "heretics" from that of the Church Fathers, or even from that of the apostolic writers, since St. Paul tells us that they are to be avoided. The story goes that St. John, when he was at the baths one day, saw Cerinthus the Gnostic coming, and fled, crying out, "Away! The pillars will fall! Cerinthus, the enemy of truth, is come into the house!" That was the traditional attitude toward heretics: avoid them. But now we associate with them, question them, talk to them. The Commissions will have to do the same. It will be difficult, no doubt, but the Council will have to come to it if its ultimate objectives are to be achieved.

The Council has opened up astonishing possibilities throughout the world, and especially in the Catholic world, for a sympathetic and positive approach to these questions. It is true that, long before the proclamation of the Council, the ecumenical cause was seen as having largely outgrown the specialized circles where it began, and as really starting to reach the mass of Chris-

tian people. Today this fact is evident. Recently, when
I was in Lille for Unity Week, I paid a visit to Cardinal
Lienart. He said to me: "What I want now is for the
idea of ecumenism to become part of the pastoral effort
of every parish."

Ecumenism is on the way to becoming a regular fea-
ture of the Church's work, just as happened not so
many years ago with Catholic Action. You will remember there was resistance to this at one time (and
there are still a few late-comers who do not know it
exists), but now priests have accepted, in general, this
recent development of the laity taking its place in the
apostolic organizations of the Church. Such an attitude
required a kind of conversion on the priests' part, a
change of approach, the introduction of a new dimension into their pastoral work. It is something of this
sort that is happening now with ecumenism. Plainly,
with the climate that the Pope has made for it and the
impulse he has given it, the Council is enabling us to
see more progress in a few months than we should
otherwise have done in three years, or even in ten.

3. The essential problems in the Church of today
are not so much the classical problems of organization
or dogma. *The burning issue is the confrontation of
Christians, laymen and priests, with their responsibilities in the world,* starting from the consciousness they
have attained of the demands of the Gospel. There is
far more concern now with choices to be made, answers
to be given: peace, Algeria, strikes, modern unbelief,

modern culture, the adaptation of Christian modes of
expression to the contemporary world, etc. In a word,
the essential problems are those of the Christian's confrontation with the world, which he faces as a consequence of his desire for absolute fidelity to the Gospel's
standards. When all is quiet on the Church's frontiers
(when a people, for example, is one hundred per cent
Christian, or the Church herself is not being questioned), interest centers on internal matters. Arguments
arise concerning clericalism and anticlericalism, laity
and priesthood, regular and secular orders, and a whole
group of similar problems that the Middle Ages were
full of. But, when the Church has the feeling of being
in the minority, is being sharply questioned by the
world, and is faced with responsibilities that have to
be undertaken in the world, then the tension is no
longer felt inside the Church, between her different
component groups, but between the Church and the
world itself. Under those conditions, laymen and clergy
find themselves involved in the same movement, concerned with the same tasks, under the necessity of
collaborating, and better still, in an ardent and happy
mood for collaboration. That is what is happening now.

All of this has important consequences for ecumenical problems too, because, after all, the problems facing
Christian people in relation to the world are pretty
much the same everywhere. Whenever we take as the
subject of our meetings with Protestants, not dogmatic
questions but pastoral ones (as, for example, a few
weeks ago at Taizé, when a dozen bishops met forty

pastors), if the spiritual climate is favorable, it soon becomes clear that the problems are almost identical. And, in spite of the very great structural differences between Christian communities, we find that our answers are often similar; in any case, we discover that our essential points of reference are the same, based as they are on Holy Scripture as the pattern for our actions.

Finally, the biggest of our current problems is to reinvent Christian man—to find a theology that is not cut across by anthropology, and an anthropology that is not in direct opposition to theology. If the things we say so often give the impression of being devitalized, I believe it is essentially because, as a rule, we do not talk about God in such a way that *man* is brought into the picture in the things we are saying about God. Theophilus of Antioch, one of the apologetical Fathers of the third century, has a thought I am very fond of. In a little book called *To Autolicos,* Autolicos the pagan says to Theophilus the Christian, "Show me your God," and Theophilus replies, "Show me your man, and I will show you my God." In this answer there is the deep sentiment that one cannot conceive the Christian God without being a Christian man. There is no Christian God unless there is a Christian man. We are coming back to the same idea today, and it is tremendously important.

I have made a considerable study of the history of Church doctrine, and it seems to me that, at the present time, we are traveling in the opposite direction from the movement of history of the fourth century until now. In the past, the movement of thought always proceeded from causes to effects, from the center to the periphery, from God or Christ to the Church herself, and, in the Church, progressively downwards and more and more into her particular organizations. From the idea of the grace of God, for instance, thinking passed to an extremely refined elaboration (useful and beautiful no doubt, but very remote) of the sacraments and the conditions and means of grace. Now, it seems, we are taking the path that leads back from means to ends, from the periphery to the center, from the Church to Christ. This could have immense ecumenical consequences.

Interpreting the Facts

From the last remark we can make a natural transition to the interpretation of the facts. We are far less concerned at the present time with a consideration of the Church in herself than with seeing the Church in vertical relationship to her source which is Christ and his Gospel, or in horizontal relationship to other Christians. To me, this is characteristic of our contemporary consciousness.

"Vertically," the Church has to re-examine herself in the light of (and in relation to) her sovereign principle. We might call this "resourcement." The word is Péguy's, and for him it means tracing one's way back along a stream, a source. For us, it is rather a return *to the source.* But these two images, in their different

ways, are really pointing to the same thing: we must always re-examine the source, the principle. We do something like this in a retreat. What, in fact, is a retreat? It is a turning back to the principles of one's existence, a getting rid of the kind of day-to-day involvement that leaves no time for anything else, except the devaluation of our convictions, the eating away of our generosity under the stress of living; it is putting oneself under the judgment of principles, of those supreme truths that we claim to be the truths of our lives, but which we so often forget in practice.

This is what the Church needs to do—go into retreat. The Council ought to be a time of retreat for the Church, a time to re-examine herself as she faces her responsibilities in the world of 1962, in the light of the principles that she accepts as the pattern of her life: the Gospel, the revelation of God, and the demands of Jesus Christ. The question is not one of the Church modifying her principles, but of re-examining her deepest principle; not of undertaking revolution, but reform. The reform of the Church means the reinterrogation of the profoundest principles of her existence. (Here, of course, we are on the outskirts of a vast domain: what it is that changes in the Church, and what does not change. The subject is a difficult one to elucidate, but it is evident that there is something in the Church which never changes, and something else which is always changing.) To tell the truth, the Catholic Church dislikes talking about reform; it is a word that jars on her ear after an unhappy experience that she had in the sixteenth century. In spite of this, however, she never ceases to reform. Are we not always hearing the complaint, "They are changing our religion"?

Next, there is the horizontal dimension, in which it is the Church's business to take account of others. After the re-examination of principles, we turn toward others, we begin a dialogue. But dialogue, as C. Santamaria has said, has two enemies: monologue and confusion. Confusion happens when everybody talks at once; monologue, when somebody is talking alone. Dialogue presupposes that someone is listening, answering, and asking questions. The longer I live, the more certain I become that one of the essentials for healthy human living, quite independently of any ecumenical or Christian perspective, is to realize and to take account of the fact that *others exist* as persons, that they too are centers around which a world is built, a world of enterprise, sorrows, joys, and hopes.

An Anglican author has written something which seems to me to express the exact antithesis of the will to dialogue: "After all, Rome only wants us as fuel for her ecclesiastical machine." This says very precisely, in a humorous way, what it is that has stopped, and still does stop, so many travelers on the road to Rome: the feeling that Rome does not like people for themselves, but simply wants to use them as machine fodder, to have one more group, one more see, under her domination. It is really this that stops people, and we have to recognize the fact. Sometime, Rome ought to ask herself seriously, "Since there's so much mistrust of me, could there be a reason?" What a step forward we shall have made when we get to that point —when we know that the others are individuals, people, and not just fuel to make us into the only center of constructive work in the world!

There is still another grave duty ahead of us, arising from a different aspect of truth. I have often noticed the kind of joy that is felt by some Christians when the prospect of a step toward understanding opens up, without the necessity for any change on their part. Every one would like to reunite, provided he does not have to sacrifice his own particularism. But surely it is clear that, if all of us remain within the bounds of our own particularism, nothing can happen at all. I am going to explain the changes that are taking place, on a deeper and more real level than might superficially be supposed.

Undoubtedly there is a legitimate side to particularism, because the grace of God has endowed different races with different religious spirits, and a variety of possibilities for resonance and revelation. Nothing of that must be lost. There can never be a sufficient variety of hymns to describe the plenitude of Jesus Christ. From another angle, however, this particularism, the insistence on keeping one's own tradition, on losing nothing that has been handed down by one's forefathers, is to be criticized and must give way.

Before 1939, ecumenical dialogue made use of a formula which, I think, is still valid. It is not being used so much today, but I should be glad to see it revived: "We have to take very seriously the questions that we put to one another." For example, the Protestants say to us, "Are you taking seriously the free gift of the grace of God? When you talk about the sacraments, the means of grace, and so many 'practices' on top of the sacraments, are you taking seriously the fact that grace is never a thing, but always the smile of God himself, and the free gift of his own good will?" (We do indeed sometimes speak of "grace" as though it were a liquid we could pour into little cups, or of "grace" attached to this or that, as if God were attached to a scapular or a medal.) "Aren't you too optimistic in your Christian arguments, your way of looking at the creation, and so on?" Pastor Pierre Maury once quoted to me St. Anselm's words: "Thou hast not yet weighed the terrible weight of sin." And on our side we must say to our brothers of the Reformation, "Have you taken in total seriousness the reality of the Body of Christ, the *ecclesia*, which, as the visible Church, has continued down from the Apostles? and the apostolicity of the ministry? and some of the texts in St. John about eternal life being already in us? That is the meaning of ecumenical dialogue."

On the basis of this dialogue and on the previous basis of a re-examination of the sources that we are all at work on in our own households, ecumenism is a call to conversion in depth. It has nothing at all to do with making concessions to one another, with half measures, with meeting each other at the lowest common denominator.

There was a bit of that in the pre-1939 brand of ecumenism. At the Edinburgh Conference in 1937, the representatives of the member churches of the Faith and Order Movement agreed on a certain number of formulas, the terms of which were purposely left rather vague in order to allow a consensus about a doctrinal minimum. This point of view is now out-of-date in the Ecumenical Movement. On the contrary, we are now looking for something greater to come out of the progress on all sides; and this is the result of going deeper down and finding the basic things that have to be discovered or rediscovered.

These rediscoveries are being made everywhere today, at any rate among Protestants and Catholics. In Protestantism, quite evidently, there has been the discovery, or rediscovery, of a certain number of "Catholic" truths which were labelled as such, and from which on that account one kept at the greatest possible distance. They range from things that seem to us very ordinary, right down to the deepest levels. A few weeks ago, a friend of mine, a Pastor at Montpellier, said to me, "You cannot imagine what it has meant to us of the Cevennes, Huguenots, Protestants of the toughest kind, to admit that there could be set forms of common prayer. Prayers like that were considered 'Catholic,' and so we had to keep away from them. Now, we are using them." This is a step, even if it still seems to us a very modest

one. There are others more important: the rediscovery
of sacramentalism, of Holy Communion; there is the
fact—a miracle, in my view—of Taizé; the rediscovery
of the religious life in its real, traditional form, although
it has been found by starting from the principles of the
Reformation and in the framework of the Reformation;
there has been some rediscovery of the idea of tradition.
In short, a great number of themes have revived, which,
fifteen years ago or even less, were the subject of real
phobias in many Protestant minds, because they were
"Catholic" ideas, and hence to be excluded.

Among ourselves there has been a return, let us say,
to the Gospel. We are recentering ourselves around
the essentials of religion, which has too often been
scattered in the side chapels (a candle here, a candle
there, a litany somewhere else, a little prayer in front
of the statue of St. Anthony or St. Joseph). I have made
some historical study of that most necessary and admirable Catholic revival of the nineteenth century,
which sought expression to a great extent along devotional lines. Most significant in this connection are
the vast numbers of religious congregations founded at
that time under the patronage of "Providence," of the
"Holy Family," of "The Child Jesus," of "St. Joseph,"
etc. The "Months" of Mary, St. Joseph, the Sacred
Heart, and the Rosary were also started then. It was
a century of devotions to the human aspects of the
Christian realities. Since I like tolerance, I have no
difficulty in justifying these devotions as a whole, in
principle. But certainly there are more central, and

deeper, things. What we are rediscovering at the moment is the thing I have taken the liberty of calling *the religious significance of faith,* a religion feeding directly on the central mysteries of salvation, which are themselves centered on the Lord's resurrection and ours. That goes very far. I believe it is going exactly along the lines of what the sixteenth-century reformers wanted and of what is authentic in their approach. We are creating a new axis for religion around the religious significance of faith, the faith in a living God. And from this comes the Christian man I was talking about a little while ago, who starts from the demands of the Gospel and faces the demands of our time, who takes his responsibilities in the world, from Jesus Christ and because of Jesus Christ.

It is this movement that is coming about now. This is the spiritual situation of our age. It must continue and intensify, and that requires a particular and absolutely indispensable religious climate.

Such a religious climate implies, as its foremost value, *patience.* This word must not be taken to mean the faculty of accepting a chronologically measurable period of delay (this is so unimportant; what does it matter if one waits for six months or two years?), but to indicate a particular quality of spirit, a spiritual attitude. This kind of patience springs from true humility, which does not consist in putting ourselves lower than we should, but, on the contrary, in putting ourselves in exactly the right place. This humble patience is made of a total renouncing of self-justification, and has the opposite disposition that opens us to penetration by other things.

Moreover this effort will have to be accomplished in a great *spirit of faith.* Ecumenism does not ask for *less,* but *more,* faith. We must not think of faith simply in its meaning of a force of intrepidity and courage in our undertakings, but in the more theological and biblical sense of the word: the unconditional offering of ourselves to God's call, or God's demands, without knowing where they will lead, and without even wanting to know where they will lead. Thus Abraham, the time-honored father of all believers, was called to leave his own country and his own kindred to go "into the land that I will show thee." He did not know where this land was, and did not seek to know. This is faith: the unlimited credit that I open to God in my life, so that he can reign there and lead me on, where he knows I have to go, without my trying myself to know where I am going. It is a surplus of this kind of faith that is needed for ecumenism. And that is as it should be, because ecumenism is an enterprise of faith, a chapter of sacred history, and not a human enterprise demanding competent, well-organized people, and all of the rest of it. It is an enterprise similar to the apostolate, of the order of the history of salvation, which supposes that God comes to awaken consciences and lead them where he wills. Under these conditions, unity, if it is eventually given us, will not be the victory of one confession, not even for the Catholic Church—although as a Catholic, I like to think that unity will take place in the apostolic Body, in the apostolic continuity, of the Church. No, unity will not be the confessional victory of a Church which would be content to assimilate others without changing anything in herself—those others who might finally have integrated with her after orbiting about her for so long. It will be a victory for Jesus Christ; a victory of the plenitude of the Gospel over Churches which have recognized this plenitude by deepening their own faith.

Under these conditions, it is clear that *prayer* is not an adventitious activity for ecumenism, a work of supererogation, but that it constitutes its very basis and is indispensable. Exactly indeed as it constitutes the basis of apostolate, if by that is meant not merely propaganda or organization, but really the celebration of a supernatural mystery, of a chapter of the history of salvation, it is clear that prayer is an absolute necessity, not only for a well-disposed heart, so that God may give us his light, but, in a deeper sense, as the fundamental reality of what we are trying to do.

I would like to say a word here about a minor debate that has been going on during the last few months. Father Charles Boyer, to whom the cause of ecumenism owes so much, published an article some months ago in which he criticized Abbé Couturier's formula: "The unity that God wills, when he wills, and in the way that he wills." Substantially what Father Boyer said was this:

We Catholics must have a kind of prayer that is expressly Catholic, that wholly corresponds to our convictions, and is therefore confessionally more specific than this formula which leaves everything to God, as though the page were blank and we were asking him to write on it. There is a definite dogmatic presupposition to our Catholic ecumenical work. For us, the question of unity is not entirely or essentially an open question, but one that has already received decisive elements of its answer.

Personally, this discussion hardly interests me, because for me, prayer for unity is only a moment, a single aspect, of prayer in general. What does it mean to pray? It is essentially to place ourselves in God's plan, to harmonize our wills with God's will, as we say in the first three petitions of the Lord's Prayer: "Hallowed be thy name. Thy kingdom come. Thy will be done. . . ." That is prayer: a communion of our wills with God's; committing ourselves to his plan; opening and offering ourselves to be the men and women that he wants, to do what he wants. Under these conditions, I do not find it necessary to be specific about my prayer. My prayer for unity is to place myself in God's hands, to offer myself to be the man he wants, to do what he wants. For that, I do not have to renounce a single one of the dogmatic convictions of my Catholicism; but neither do I feel the need of making my prayer specific by bringing a theology into it that does not contradict the prayer, and moreover, is not contradicted by it.

These few reflections have had no other aim but to help us to find our bearings, to have a better understanding on the level of ideas—and also on the level of the knowledge of God's will—of what is happening at this moment. Exactly where this meeting is leading us, we obviously cannot know. But it seems absolutely unthinkable that such vast preparations should lead to nothing. The rest we can leave to God.

6

School for Ecumenists

Why Be Concerned with Ecumenism?

More and more, large numbers of Christians are asking themselves, "What can we do for Christian unity?" They ask the question because they have the feeling that something is happening. And it is. A movement has been started in the world by the Spirit of God. Christians, that is to say, people who want to give their lives to Jesus Christ as the Apostles taught us to know him, these same Christians whom history has divided, are seeking to abolish the scandal of their oppositions, and even, if possible, of their divisions. For if there is one Lord and one salvation, there ought to be one Church—which does not at all mean uniformity in every respect! There are legitimate differences of rites, of customs, and even of theological formulations of the same profound faith. This explains why, right from the beginning, there was an Eastern Church and a Western Church, fundamentally the same and yet very different.

WHAT IS ECUMENISM?

We call "ecumenism" (from a Greek word meaning "world-wide") the sum-total of the efforts that are being made for the reintegration of Christians into the unity of a single Church. A part of this effort has been organized in the form of a World Council of Churches, to which, however, the Catholic Church does not belong.

Although we formerly quarrelled, cursed, banished, and sometimes very cruelly killed one another, today we are trying, first to understand the ancient grievances, because many of them were real and had a meaning; and then, as each of us delves deeper into the truth, we can engage in a dialogue with all those who, from their own sides, are seeking the same goal. Our roads must finally converge toward a point of light where we can communicate in total fidelity to him whom we all acknowledge as our Lord, and in the gift that he has made us of his New Dispensation.

WIDENING HORIZONS

If we are now once again trying to find each other like this, instead of rejecting each other, is it because our love of truth or our convictions are weakening? Not at all. The irenic (that is, peaceful and cordial) or ecumenical attitude proceeds from the same love of truth which formerly engendered intolerance, but the love is differently applied. Then, they looked only at the letter of orthodoxy, and could not admit any particle of truth as existing outside it. Naturally, no Catholic can admit that dogma could be mixed with error, or heresy be regarded as truth. But we realize better today that this point of view, true though it may be, does not exhaust the truth.

It is not out of false liberalism or from a skeptical or relativist attitude toward truth that we are tolerant. It is not in order to admit falsehood that we are engaging in dialogue with "heretics"; it is out of a desire to grasp a truth that is more complete, more luminously explained. Why? Precisely because, in our investigations, we are striving to go further, and by ways that are purer, in order to be able to remove from our brothers the reasons which they said they had for not accepting with us—and we with them—a doctrine that they felt had gone astray from, or was incomplete in its correspondence with, the revelation and the work of salvation of God.

INCREASING RESPONSIBILITIES

"But what can we do about it?" Many Catholics will ask themselves this question. They regard themselves not as teaching, but as taught, members of the Church; in any case they are not specialists in such matters.

The objection evidently has a grain of truth. Everywhere culture is spreading and life is becoming more complicated at the same time. But it is also more and more apparent that to be Christians we must be intelligent; that is to say, we must use the intelligence we have. One fact, at any rate, is striking about the most wide-awake of the faithful today: their sense of their responsibilities; their desire to use their time in a Christian way. They want to belong to God, but in a way that does not prevent them from belonging to the world. They want a spirituality that is not, so to speak, half-way between earth and heaven, but one that is involved with concrete action and requires them to relate their action to God.

For a Christian today, to accept his times is to engage himself usefully in a society which is not that of the Middle Ages, ruled almost like a monastery, but a divided society, wedded to technique, a postrevolutionary society (post-French and post-Russian Revolutions), postcolonial and postpaternal. It is also a post-Reformation society. We have to accept as Christians the fact of Christian divisions, as God asks us to accept it, with the heavy heritage of the past and its liabilities. This demands patience of us, and hope for new possibilities, and prayer and effort.

Working toward union itself requires that everyone should be interested in it—just as does working toward peace. From the moment when we form a group we become answerable for one another. The behavior of one member or one part of the group is imputed to the group as a whole, particularly if it is a matter for criticism. Thus we often see the finest and broadest efforts toward peace reduced to nothing in a single moment, by a regrettable incident, a word, an unfriendly gesture. What has been gained with such difficulty at one level can so easily be lost at another. The most beautiful, the most valid explanations that our

Protestant friends would be ready and glad to wel-
come can be silenced by the behavior of some retarded
member of that same Catholicism—consisting more of
practices than of faith—against which the Reformation
was a protest. I well remember once giving a talk in
which my Protestant audience had found nothing but
what was honest, Christian, and acceptable, although
it was entirely Catholic. They were impressed. But on
the way out of the hall there were some people, with
the best of intentions but considerably less enlightenment, handing out illustrated leaflets recommending
some pious practice, accompanied by prayers with indulgences attached to them, that I myself would have
had no wish at all to say. My lecture was ruined.

ECUMENISM, THE AFFAIR OF ALL
CHRISTIAN PEOPLE

What happened on a small scale on that evening is
happening on a much larger one every day. The whole
Church is answerable for the ecumenical effort. To a
tiny and yet very real extent, the issue is in the hands
of one parishioner in some remote village. To make
peace, specialists are needed: diplomats and experts.
But the work of diplomats and experts comes to nothing if it is not supported by the will and the hopes of
ordinary people. What is the use of negotiations if people remain bellicose, or of words if the situation itself
is still inflamed? In the same way, the whole Church
must undertake the ecumenical effort, just as she does
missionary or reforming efforts, everyone co-operating

with the leaders or the specialists on whom the responsibility for action particularly rests.

What Can We Do for Unity?

CHANGE THE CLIMATE

Newman says that, when he was a boy and saw the French prisoners from Waterloo being marched through the streets of London, he stepped down from the pavement and lifted the greatcoat of one of them to see whether he had a tail. The small boy who had written in his school dictionary, opposite the word "Antichrist," the word "Pope," thought that papists had tails. One could quote many such stories, some of them no older than yesterday or the day before. We are coming back from afar, but we are coming back. A Protestant lady, eighty years old, a close friend of my family, said quite spontaneously a little while ago, "It isn't like it used to be. When I was a child, I was almost the only Protestant in my village, and the other children used to call me names and jeer. Now, we at least respect each other, and there's even cordiality."

It is a pleasure to hear something like that. But since, in human affairs, everything has its good and its bad side, some disadvantages are mixed with this good. A friend of mine, an archpriest in a locality where there are a good many Protestants, who also enjoy a majority status in social esteem, was telling me that one of his parishioners had been married at the Protestant church. When he reminded her of the rules of Catholic discipline, she answered, "I said to myself, now that our priest and the pastor agree, it's all the same." I told this story later to a pastor friend, in quite a different part of the country, and he said, "I had another case like that. She had the same thought, too."

ECUMENICAL EDUCATION OF THE FAITHFUL

These things do not prevent us from seeking fraternal peace. They simply show that, when we begin to have esteem for one another and engage in dialogue, there must be simultaneous education of the faithful. This will be pure gain. And besides, there is still so much to be done! We have tremendous liabilities, and they should be assessed clearly, because, in the psychological field, discovering and naming the malady is half-way to curing it.

It is very important for us to grasp this fact: we are never engaged with others—and, in the past, we have hardly ever been so engaged—purely and simply *as a Church*, but always as part of our society. This society has existed for long centuries in the West, and has its own ingrained habits, forms of expression, social situations involving honors and privileges, etc. All this, and often without being fully aware of it, we have taken with us into the mission field along with our Christianity, with the result that now the latter is being questioned wherever European influence is questioned. And again, where our relationships as divided Christians are concerned, we meet each other with a past that, to a certain extent, determines our forms of thought and our reactions. But the "others" also have a past different from ours, and hence we do not understand one another. Besides, in the pattern of our past, on both sides there have been moments of rivalry, of opposition, and sometimes of violent war, intolerance, and ugly practices. The spectacle of these oppositions —the Thirty Years' War in Germany, the wars of religion in France and England—has historically been one of the most powerful causes of modern atheism. Religions, including the religion of Christ, have appeared essentially as divisive influences, inspiring intolerance and violence. The principles of peace and unity have been sought elsewhere.

THE ROLE OF NONTHEOLOGICAL FACTORS

From all this it follows that we cannot see or approach one another except through an isolating and distorting screen of ideas, habits, prejudices, and feelings. For more than twenty years now, the Ecumenical Movement has been studying these so-called "nontheological factors" of division. The term designates those habits of thought and collective situations of historical origin which, although never mentioned in the lists of our doctrinal divergences, are, in practice at least, as influential as these in keeping us at a distance and making it painful for us to meet. It can sometimes happen that the nontheological factors are more powerful than the doctrinal ones, and even that they are the real motives for division. And where doctrinal factors are at work, they are reinforced by the others with all the strength of instinct or passion, all the power of *esprit de corps*.

This is so in the case of the opposition between Eastern and Western Christianity. Often the non-theological factors are more influential where religious convictions have become less personal and less intense. We know of numbers of Protestants who never go to church, who are sometimes not even aware of the name of their pastor, but for whom, to become a Catholic, or to marry a Catholic, or to have Catholic children would be unthinkably horrible. As one of these mothers said to her daughter, "I would have preferred you to turn Jew. It would have been less of a humiliation."

SOME COMPLEXES

An inveterate situation of noncontact may also of itself be a substantive cause of separation. It is the same in human relations, and is the story of more than one quarrel. There has been some trivial disagreement or offense, but the parties have not recovered from the upset. The days have gone by, and soon it is a long time since there was any sort of friendly exchange, since a kindly word was said or deed done. And now, the real motive for their not seeing each other is that they are not seeing each other. From there it is only one step to mutual distrust and mutual attribution of inimical feelings.

The most serious result of this situation has been the creation of a number of complexes, of which the most destructive is the complex of distrust. Distrust in a man's heart is something as deep and as inhibiting as the feeling of injustice which touches consciousness at the very center of its existence. It is useless to make advances or propose really just and generous solutions if there is no trust; everything, even the best, that is done is simply attributed to cunning ruses or the blackest of designs. How many times have we not had the experience—and our Protestant and Orthodox brothers could no doubt give similar examples, working in the opposite direction—that an explanation we have made twenty times over has not been accepted, perhaps not even understood, and our interpretation of a text has been rejected. But then, if I quote a passage from Luther, or Calvin, or one of the Greek Fathers, there is immediate agreement. The other man has been reassured. Distrust is often the attitude and the defense of the weak. The same can be said of intolerance. The following are additional reasons why the Christian life, now more than ever, demands intelligence: it is imposing on us confrontation and dialogue, and one cannot prudently engage in these unless he is strong. How true, as always, is that witty observation of Father Mersch: "It is because they have no skeletons that certain animals surround themselves with shells."

THE ANTI-ROMAN COMPLEX

Among the complexes that other people have about us, and in close relationship with the distrust that I have just been mentioning, there is the notorious anti-Roman complex. With varying shades in the details of its motivations and expressions, it appears to be common to the Orthodox East and the Protestant West. It is a very profound reality. We may wonder whether it is Christian, even while not excluding the idea that it may be deeply motivated by attachment to authentic Christian values (if sometimes wrongly interpreted ones). I believe it would be possible to find a formula for these values and for their disputable interpretation at the same time in Dostoievsky's "Legend of the Grand Inquisitor" (*The Brothers Karamazov*, Book V, Chapter 5). I had been a priest for just a year when a Protestant pastor from Berlin and, only a few weeks later, an Orthodox friend in Paris, each named this creation of Dostoievsky's genius as the quintessential expression of their grievances. It seems likely that the attribution has some truth.

Should we not take note of it, we Catholics? Should we not give ourselves the benefit of this lucidity, and question ourselves honestly, humbly, about the reasons for this monumental fact, the persistence of which historically has been expressed in thousands of actions and records? Rome is distrusted. Men attribute to her the aims of domination and sentiments of paternalism that put them on the defensive and make them keep their distance, even though many outside the bounds of Catholicism are prepared to recognize the benefits the papacy has conferred on Christianity and on the world.

Educational Suggestions

Here are a few real and practical suggestions for co-operating toward the elimination of the complexes of distrust, the situation of noncontact, and the nontheo-logical factors of division, and for achieving that trans-formation of climate which, thanks be to God, has already begun in earnest.

FORM THE HABIT OF RESPECT FOR OTHERS

Respect for others must begin in childhood, with edu-cation. Here, I should like to offer a personal testi-mony to the advantages which seem to me to result from Catholic children having Protestant or Jewish friends and companions while they are young. When the family educational climate is based on a whole-somely positive Christian point of view, this mixing of friendships brings no danger of syncretism (mixing of doctrine) or of liberalism; on the contrary, it offers the great advantages of initiation into the interlocutory structure of the human community and of Christian-ity itself. We must also draw attention to another important point concerning education in the awareness of others: the words that are used in speaking about them. Without our being conscious of it, they are the carriers of a whole spiritual attitude. When I am thinking about the existence of others or talking about them, if I give them comical or half-contemptuous nicknames, I am putting my thoughts into a frame-work which, from the very first, will distort these thoughts to forms of disparagement. It is then proba-ble that the mental picture I shall make of others and through which I shall see them will be similarly warped. All hate-propaganda uses pictures and terms like these, which have assured effects. We need to watch carefully the words we use in our school books, and even those we use in our everyday speech.

KNOWING, AND BEING INFORMED

All Catholic workers for unity have first made serious efforts to inform themselves. At the present time the specialized Catholic magazines are giving the best reports of the Ecumenical Movement; the quality of the information they provide about the "others" has often been praised by the others themselves. At the end of this article some practical indications for the use of nonspecialists will be found. It is indispensable to have some valid elementary information about the Reformers, contemporary Protestantism, and the Eastern Church. The annual celebration of the Week of Prayer is an occasion for giving this information in parishes and schools. It can be done through lectures, the distribution of leaflets, articles in the press and parish magazines, and exhibitions. Every day, for example, there can be an explanatory talk linked to a subject for prayer: on the Eastern Church, Lutheranism, Calvinism, Anglicanism, the Ecumenical Movement, missions, current efforts towards union, etc.

DO NOT NEGLECT IMPORTANT CHANCES OF
BRINGING ENLIGHTENMENT OR OF
ESTABLISHING TRUTH

It is certainly very difficult to have an appreciation of one's own situation in comparison with someone else's. Every one is a bad judge of his own cause. My feelings on this subject, therefore, must be expressed with reserve. I would prefer to believe that Catholics are mostly *ignorant* about the others, and that the others have *false ideas* or *prejudices* about Catholicism. I would not favor, and would rather advise against, the idea of anyone setting himself up, in season and out of season, as a righter of wrongs and a controversialist. We would make ourselves odious by so doing, and slip into hard and narrow spiritual attitudes, as though we were in possession of ready-made truth, and had not the virtue of welcoming acceptance. This is not Christian. We must always seek to be possessed by the truth, and live with the feeling that we have to be converted; and are, therefore, also open to receive. Indeed, in all dialogue, we receive at least as much as we give. But we shall, on occasion, also be prepared to criticize calmly and firmly a wrong interpretation, to explain our Church's position and show her real attitude, suggest the truth that has been misunderstood by those to whom we are speaking, and recommend such and such a book, or article, or lecture as being able to clear up the difficulty and do some good. In all this we should try our hardest to choose the *positive* moment for explanation, and to prevent the discussion from turning into controversy. To build up, to put one stone on top of another, is much better than to empty a truckload of stones haphazardly, with the possibility of crushing or wounding someone else.

BUILD BRIDGES, CREATE CONTACTS

At least we should try to profit from the occasions of this kind that life may offer. Speaking at the Protestant Kirchentag at Munich on August 16, 1959, Professor Theodore Heuss, former President of the Federal Republic, welcomed the Catholics who were present. He said that all his life he had had friends amongst them, and he expressed the wish that all his coreligionists might have the same experience. And, indeed, the experience that Theodore Heuss had in the highest position in the state can be shared by many more in the humbler places that they occupy. Many do share it (in particular, in France, in the educational world). There are numerous occasions for working together in the domains of charity, of helping sufferers, or aiding underdeveloped countries; or in trade union, civic, or political activities; or again in protest movements or demonstrations that may be inspired by the demands of the Christian conscience. All these are occasions for us to meet one another on ground where we shall discover ourselves as Christians, in spite of certain differences, even serious ones, in our dogmatic ideas. Hence also, they are occasions for us to learn to esteem one another, and, without denying any of our own convictions, to appreciate the *positive Christianity* in others. With this as our starting point, we shall be able to look for a unanimity that denies no fragment of the sacred repository of truth, and in which all its existing and still scattered parts will find fulfillment.

*Carrying the Great Intention of Unity
in a Heart of Prayer*

Prayer makes the Christian, for it is like the breathing
of the soul which has given itself, by faith, to the living God. It is the prayer of Christian individuals and
communities that forms the urns of love in which souls
are carried by the communion of saints. The work
of the Church, like all Christian endeavor, is a *spiritual*
work. It does not arise from the world of human en-
terprises and their returns, but from a ministry of the
mercy of God, whose loving will it is that men should
be saved. It does not arise from human diplomacy;
although it has elements of discussion and negotiation
which resemble those of politics, these are only its
human features, real indeed and necessary, but not its
profoundest nor its most decisive aspects. Nothing spiritual can be conceived or brought to birth except through
the Holy Spirit. The realization of unanimity can come
only from this source, for without doing violence to
consciences it inclines them from within in the direction of communion; hence the unbelievable miracle of
concord between opposing Christians, each one of whom
engages his powerful religious fidelity to preserve the
inheritance of his forebears and his Church.

PRAYER IS EFFECTIVE

Prayer is effective because it brings about a condition
that God wants us to reach, in response to his grace, in
order to achieve his plan of salvation. It does not change

God's mind, but enters into what he expects from us, so that his will may be done on earth, in human history, as it is in heaven. If St. John Chrysostom was able to write, "The man who prays has his hand on the rudder of the world," how much more must this be true of the prayer "that they may be one," which, in the spirit and the words of John 17, rests on the prayer of Jesus himself?

PRAYER BANISHES DISTRUST

We do not always receive what we ask for in prayer, or we do not receive it in the way we had imagined or hoped. But there is one fruit of prayer that is always certain: it changes our hearts. We do not come out of it exactly the same as we went in. If others are involved in our prayer—because we are praying for them or with them—our relationships with these others are completely transformed by it. Praying for someone else, an "enemy" for instance, or someone who has wronged us, opens possibilities in our hearts that would never have revealed themselves without that prayer. Praying *with* someone establishes a first bond of communion, opens our eyes, and banishes distrust.

This is the experience I have had in our meetings with Protestants or Orthodox. Prayer does not replace doctrinal confrontation, but allows it to be exercised in a less polemic and more intellectual atmosphere, with confidence and the feeling of being called to a common work.

JURISPRUDENCE REGARDING COMMON PRAYER

The common prayer of Christians belonging to different communions is naturally subject to certain rules. This is not a matter of regimentation or of narrowness, because the official rules of the Catholic Church are remarkably broad in this respect; it is a matter of the loyalty of each individual to his own Church. And also it is a matter of honesty about the fact of disunion, a burden whose harsh consequences we cannot easily or cheaply overcome, but which we must bear just as it is.

A Catholic may not, in any circumstances of normal life, actively take part in the public worship of a dissident communion as such; practically, he may not take part in the celebration of its sacraments and above all in its Eucharist. To do so would be to commit the fault of *Communicatio in sacris* (*in divinis*), or liturgical communion. Two restrictions in the foregoing statement need to be explained:

1. "In any circumstances of *normal* life." This is because the Church admits that a Catholic in danger of death may, if no Catholic priest is available, and if there is no risk of endangering his faith or causing scandal to others, receive sacramental absolution and the Eucharistic viaticum from a priest of a schismatic Church whose orders are valid. It seems that, in face of death (or "eschatologically," as we say in technical theological terms), the barriers of legitimacy are lowered. The question of Church gives way to the spirit-

ual good of a person on the brink of eternity, that is, in face of the absolute, of which all the rules of Churches are only servants.

2. *"Actively* take part." This means, behaving exactly like a member of the other Christian communion. We could not do that without effectively belonging to the communion in question. To do so without belonging to it would be to fail in loyalty both to our own Church or communion, because we should be performing the liturgical act of worship of another confession—a sort of spiritual adultery—and to the communion concerned, because we should be performing its act of worship without really belonging to it. Nevertheless, Canon Law, which regulates the behavior of Christians in the external life of the Church, tolerates or permits, in certain cases, attendance at the public worship of other communions: it then requires that the attendance be "passive." What does this mean? It does not mean that we should not pray; even less that we should assume an attitude that might shock or offend the faithful whose worship we are attending; it would be better by far to stay at home. It means that we should not perform all the acts of the public worship of others as the others themselves perform them.

The motive in these permitted cases must be some serious reason of relationship or representation, if the function we are exercising requires it: for example, attendance at a baptism, a marriage, or a funeral service. Doubtful cases should be referred to a bishop (can.

1258, n. 2). We think that the motive of ecumenical study or participation in an ecumenical meeting under proper conditions can be classed among these serious reasons, provided there is no danger either of scandal or perversion (two conditions that can easily be justified by our Lord's warnings: Matt. 5:29-30, and 18:6-9). But simple curiosity would certainly not be enough to warrant such participation. Similarly, a Catholic cannot be the godfather, in the liturgical sense of the word, at a non-Catholic baptism, or a witness at a wedding. We must understand that this prohibition is something quite different from regimentation or narrowness. These are cases in which Christians must, as we have said, take up and carry the burden of the drama of disunity, and find their own spiritual attitudes in the reflection of its sombre light. The simplest thing is to explain in this way the refusal that one is obliged to give, albeit with feelings of profound regret.

Although the Church is strict with regard to the whole domain of *ecclesiastical* acts, that is, acts of public worship, Christians are, on the other hand, allowed to pray together under the conditions of private life. "Private" does not here mean praying with one or two others alone and in silence, but "non-liturgical," outside liturgical public worship. Therefore we may pray together aloud in an assembly such as a study meeting or conference. The instruction *Ecclesia catholica* of December 20, 1949, which lays down the rules to be observed in such cases, expressly authorizes the recitation together of the Lord's Prayer (*Pater*) or of any other prayer approved by the Church—for example, a psalm, or even a prayer from the Missal, but outside the liturgical act itself. This often takes place even with our own bishops presiding, at ecumenical meetings or at various public events of the Week of Prayer (at the end of lectures, etc.). Prayer like this, sincerely offered up by a whole gathering, is not only most impressive; we cannot doubt that it is truly heard, for "Where two or three. . . ."

THE WEEK OF UNIVERSAL PRAYER FOR UNITY

1. *Origins.* The Week of Universal Prayer for Unity is celebrated, as you know, from the eighteenth to the twenty-fifth of January, that is, according to the Catholic calendar, from the feast of the Chair of St. Peter at Rome to that of the Conversion of St. Paul. The subjects of both these feasts have obvious ecumenical significance, and it is interesting in this connection to notice their order. We do not end with the Chair of St. Peter, but with a conversion; and while we cannot, of course, equate this with the conversion of non-Catholic confessions to the Church, we may see it as implying the spiritual conversion of all mankind to the Gospel. The Week of Prayer was instituted, as you may know, in 1908, by two Anglican ministers, the Reverend Spencer Jones and Father Paul Wattson. The latter founded a community in the United States called the Community of the Atonement—a word with the combined meanings of redemption, expiation, and rec-

onciliation. In the same year, 1908, Father Wattson entered the Catholic Church.

2. *Development in the Catholic Church.* The Week of Prayer was encouraged by a succession of popes: Pius X, Benedict XV, and Pius XI. These three had also encouraged the nine-day period of prayer for Christian reunion instituted by Leo XIII and celebrated between Ascension and Pentecost. However, the January Week soon began to take precedence over this latter period, not simply because it happens to fall at a time of the year which is relatively free from ceremonies, conferences, and meetings, but because of the underlying conception of it which has prevailed, thanks principally to Abbé Paul Couturier (d. March 24, 1953). The Week had originally been suggested *to Catholics* (or Catholic sympathizers), as a time devoted to prayer for the conversion of Christians belonging to the various dissident communions, and also of relapsed Catholics; each day had a special intention. In this form it may have represented a useful peg on which to hang conferences, but prayer could not be allowed to become specialized like this or put into compartments. Prayer must embrace every part, or rather, the *whole* of the undivided cause of Christian unity. Furthermore when prayer is truly an act that has its setting in a religious context of *faith,* there is no need for it to be specialized, like acts of devotion or comfort which are directed toward particular objects; it finds its place in the totality of the divine plan.

3. *The Week in its present form is due to Abbé Paul Couturier.* Clearly, if it were a matter of praying formally and specifically for their conversion to Catholicism, we could not invite either Anglicans, Protestants, or Orthodox to join with us in the Week of Universal Prayer for Unity. But more and more, the January Week became a time when, if they still could not pray in the unanimity of a single Church, divided Christians were fervently praying, simultaneously and conjointly, imploring God for the favor of their reunion in a single house of prayer. This fact alone of simultaneous and convergent prayer was a spiritual reality of such importance, was so much required by the development of the Ecumenical Movement, that it was essential to find the means of embodying it in a really unanimous form. The formula proposed by Abbé Paul Couturier was acceptable to everyone: the grace we should pray for is the unity that God wills, by the means that he wills.

This was not just a clever move on our part, a roundabout way of "possessing" the others. It was an honest expression of the fact that our faith and our hope are in God, and of the fact that our disunity and our reunion are a mystery whose precise architecture God alone knows, and which goes beyond anything that *we* can think we have discovered about it. It did not result from our having *less* faith, but, on the contrary, from having a great enough faith to repose our certainties and our hopes in God. It did not turn any of the dogmatic certainties into relative truths, but it left room for the margin of God's grace on the page where they are written in their human expression.

4. *The Week has become an established custom.* Today, the January Week of Prayer is fully celebrated in a great number of localities. It is introduced into the programs of groups of high school and college students. I can vouch for it, because I have been preaching, during the course of the Week, every year since 1936, in eleven or twelve towns of France and the surrounding countries. I can vouch also for the quality of the audiences and their increasing numbers, and above all for the authentic qualities of attention and religious feeling that can be felt among them. It is truly a week of grace that is given to us each year. One priest said that his parish had been transformed by it. To those who will give themselves to the experience with faith, hope, and purity of heart, we can promise the reality of the Lord's visitation, for we are wholly surrendered to his will.

Co-operating in Intellectual or Scientific Work

First of all, as we have already seen, the climate can be changed through every attempt to give valid information. This will come about among those who have teaching responsibilities, that is, among parents and teachers of every kind, by striving for authenticity when, in history or literature, subjects arise such as the Eastern "Schism," the Reformation, the Wars of Religion, etc.

A TASK RESERVED FOR SPECIALISTS

Generally speaking, everything that contributes to authenticity in Christian realities and Christian behavior is working toward reunion and has ecumenical value. For ecumenical work there must be specialists: men who have the time, the resources, the vocation, the grace, and ultimately even the official duty to work on the difficult theological and historical questions with which we are involved in ecumenical dialogue. In this as in all else, each must play his part. "God," says St. Paul, "is not a God of disorder but of peace" (1 Cor. 14:33, 40). But it is one thing to be engaged in technical work related to questions of ecumenical interest, and another to act in a way that simply has ecumenical value.

A TASK FOR ALL THE FAITHFUL

All Christian activity can (and no doubt it is permissible to say *must*) have an ecumenical value. That is to say, it should favor the unity of all the sons of God and of Jesus Christ. Every time that we achieve a more correct appreciation of a point of Christian history or doctrine, every time that we evolve for ourselves or suggest to others a more genuine conception of God, of the Gospel, and of the Church, every time that we aim at a more authentic celebration of the sacraments, at a more authentic art or style in the design of buildings for worship or in the writing of our texts (from doctrinal texts right down to church notices, tracts, and posters announcing parish activities), or in the way we formulate our prayers, etc., we are doing something that has real ecumenical value.

The field is immense; it is coextensive with the whole life of the Church. Clearly everyone can, and even must, work in it, not as a formal specialist, but as a soldier in an engagement which involves the whole Church. And again, the field is immense viewed from another aspect.

With the contemporary development of a sense of history, mention is often made of collective responsibility, or, what comes to much the same thing, historical responsibility. Leaving aside here the technical discussion of the precise limits of such a responsibility, let us suggest, in a practical fashion, an idea of the reality to which it corresponds. Just as creation is not simply an act that took place in the past, "in the beginning," a pure initial stimulus, but is continuing through the whole historical development of the universe, so also the great Christian divisions are not events that happened *once*, at a precisely assignable date; they are happening every day, in a history one moment of which we are living through, or rather, in which we are all to some extent, and for a moment, actors. The Eastern "Schism" is happening now. The Reformation is happening now. Of course these great historical realities are inseparable from certain historic situations: the Reformation did not occur in the framework of the Church of St. Augustine or of St. Gregory the Great, but in that of the Church of the sixteenth century, which was in turn conditioned by the whole period of the Middle Ages in the West, with its scholasticism, its papacy, its temporal rule of Christianity, its pilgrimages, its indulgences, etc. It is not impossible to imagine a state of the Church in which the Reformation would not have taken place, in which the terrible rent would not have occurred. Did not Von Harnack, writing on the subject of the decree on Justification carried by the Council of Trent in 1547 (eleven months after the death of Luther) say: "It is possible to doubt whether the Reformation would have developed if this decree had been carried by the Lateran Council at the beginning of the century, and if it had truly passed into the flesh and blood of the Church." ["Man kann zweifeln ob die Reformation sich entwickelt hätte, wenn dieses Dekret auf dem Laterankonzil am Anfang des Jahrhunderts erlassen worden und wirklich in Fleisch und Blut der Kirche übergegangen wäre" (*Dogbengesch.*, III, p. 711)].

The idea that we are trying to express is this: every time we behave in such a way that the rupture between the East and the West, or the split of the Reformation, become humanly and historically almost inevitable, we become coresponsible for them. Every time, on the other hand, we behave in such a way that, if men had behaved in the same way in the past, the evil of the rupture between East and West, or the tragedy of the split of the Reformation, would have been avoided, we are contributing to the healing of these same evils. That goes as much for Catholics as for their separated brothers.

TWO FORMS OF CO-OPERATION

Once again you are going to say, "I am not a specialist. What can I do?" Our responsibilities change, and
increase too, as we gain more knowledge. That is why
we shall distinguish between two broad categories: (1)
people who are not qualified in this respect; and (2)
people who have a special responsibility arising from
their more developed knowledge.

1. It is always possible to take part in the movement, to keep oneself informed, perhaps to receive or
have passed on to one a publication that has articles
on it (just as subscribing to a missionary magazine is
an effective way of becoming interested in missions).
You can ask your clergy to talk about it, to organize
something on the parish level or in Catholic groups for
the January Week. You can contribute your part to
the forming, in the Church, of public opinion and of
enlightened opinion. The faithful do not decide or direct, but they must *reasonably* express their wishes.
The history of the Church offers more than one example of important decisions or initiatives that were
taken in response to lay requests: it was Catherine of
Siena who brought about the return of the pope from
Avignon to Rome; it was a group of students who
were instrumental in the choice of Abbé Lacordaire
for the pulpit of Notre Dame. Naturally there are ways
of doing these things. The tone of demand, the application of pressure, have never been acceptable in
the Church. Good sense is only the ordinary name for

the Christian virtue of prudence. But prudence does not mean cowardice, or passivity, or flabby, weak indifference.

2. Among those who have greater possibilities, and therefore also a greater degree of moral responsibility, we may note two sorts, though often indeed they are found together in a single individual.

(a) Those who have a certain intellectual competence, perhaps even a scientific one. But the domain hardly matters because, as we have already said, all valid ecumenical work contributes to the creation of an atmosphere of authenticity in which complexes are dissolved, and which by itself alone represents an ecumenical value. If a Catholic is competent and honest in geography or mathematics, he increases the honesty of the whole body of Catholics, and makes it appear as acceptable and trustworthy in the sight of all other men, whether Christians or not. But there are privileged domains where valid work *may* have, in itself, a great and immediate ecumenical effectiveness: philosophy and history—history above all.

(b) Those among the faithful who have, properly speaking, *an ecumenical vocation,* at least in the broad sense of the word; by this we mean a call to do something special in the service of the cause of Christian unity: taking part, for instance, in a group for ecumenical meetings and work, perhaps even organizing one; or launching in one's town or parish (naturally in union and collaboration with a priest) a Week of Unity.

Traveling, as I have, about France and sometimes her neighboring countries during the second half of every January for the last twenty-five years, I know that the Week of Prayer "works" wherever there is someone who feels concerned about it, and that means someone who is giving himself to it.

RULES CONCERNING WORKING-MEETINGS WITH NON-CATHOLICS

Active participation in meetings and in work with non-Catholics—in a word, in what we may call an ecumenical group—is subject to the following rules, which were laid down in the instruction *Ecclesia catholica* of December 20, 1949. The document begins with a reminder, which hardly needs to be given to a Catholic, that the whole domain of interconfessional relations is under the supervision of the episcopate, and therefore requires the authorization either of the local bishop, if the activity in question involves only local participation, or of the Holy See, if the activity is on a national or international scale. Laymen may have meetings with non-Catholics. If these are simply on the level of friendship and personal relations, the occurrence needs no other rules than those which cover all Christian personal activity; but, if a meeting is to be formal and organized, with a confrontation in view, then the local bishop or a vicar general or the priest designated for these things in the diocese must be consulted. If there is any question of theological discussions in collaboration with Protestants, a formal authorization is required, and the bishop must be kept informed of the proceedings of the meetings.

By Way of Conclusion:
What Can We Hope for?

We can hope for everything, if the Holy Spirit is at work. "Jesus," as Father de Foucauld used to say, "is the master of the impossible." If God has really started something in the direction of Christian reunion, who is to assign limits to his work? There is only one thing for us to do: to remain faithful, and to work with all our strength in the very strength of his grace. *He* knows the outcome.

However, if we want to attempt some human supposition, we must recognize both that reunion is humanly impossible and that, in spite of this, so many things have been achieved that many more can reasonably be hoped for.

HUMANLY INSURMOUNTABLE DIFFICULTIES

Yes, reunion appears to be impossible when we look realistically at the absolute character of certain oppositions. All the more since no one can or should make concessions about the truth as he perceives it. For example, on one side there is the doctrine of papal infallibility; on the other, there is the Orthodox teaching that only those Councils are infallible in which the infallibility of the Church resides; and finally, the Reformed Churches, which refuse to attribute any legal infallibility to ecclesiastical decisions, whatever they may be. And when we think of the centuries of divergent evolution that have gone by, the inheritance of which cannot be set aside in one day, or even in several generations; when we think of the multitude of practical questions, which seem secondary only in appearance (for instance, with the East, the legislation on the indissolubility of marriage); when we think, supposing unity to have been achieved, how little it would take to reawaken ancient oppositions, when their evidences and their very words are so indelibly inscribed in the records of history—it seems obvious that, humanly speaking, unity is impossible.

THE ROAD WE HAVE ALREADY COVERED

And yet, some of the road has been covered already. Things which seemed impossible thirty or forty years ago are accomplished facts today. Even in doctrinal matters, without making concessions to a false liberalism, we have already recognized that some points over which we had quarrelled, and more, which appeared to be *decisive* points of opposition, could, if properly explained, cease to be factors of division. Thus, between East and West, the question of the Procession of the Holy Spirit (*Filioque*); and between the Reformers and ourselves, perhaps, the question of Justification. These are two points which were absolutely decisive in the disputes that led to separation. Better explained, they leave the way open for an understanding. There are other chapters, no doubt, for which explanations are possible, and will be found or elaborated. Reconciliation is taking place already in certain sectors: Scripture and Tradition, Faith and Sacraments. A concordant version of the Bible is an idea that has been gaining ground from year to year since the end of the last World War. And we might point out other significant convergences, for example, in the domain of the forms of prayer.

WORKING IN HOPE

We must not anticipate the future. Let us work. Let us pay the price of so great an undertaking: a price of labor, of prayer, of suffering, but also the price of patience or constancy, of which St. Paul says, in a way that astonishes us because we should rather have expected the contrary, that it engenders hope. "Such a hope is no mockery, because God's love has flooded our inmost heart through the Holy Spirit he has given us" (Rom. 5:4-5).

7

The Future of the Church

Consideration of the real future of the Church is eschatology, the study of what lies beyond history, of that toward which history is striving. There are the promises of eternal life—new heavens and a new earth where Justice will dwell. But here we are going to deal with the historical future of the Church on earth, during the "interim" of which the Fathers speak. I cannot agree with those who hold that predictions concerning it are impossible, since it is even up to us to prepare that future. By way of a beginning, however, it is important to set forth briefly the principles or method of determining what the prospects may be as far as the Church is concerned.

To a certain extent, predictions are entirely possible because there are some sound bases on which to make them. First of all we have a knowledge of the past, not merely from the point of view of an historian or chronicler, but also from the point of view of historical development and of an understanding of this development which, in examining the sequence of events, looks for purposes and absolutes. Father Teilhard de Chardin used to say that he studied the past in order to discover

the tendencies and main features of the future. A
knowledge of the great historical events supplies mean-
ingful clues to the farseeing intellect. How much more
so, then, does our foreknowledge of a number of facts
and conditions that will almost certainly prevail in the
world of tomorrow. We can estimate with a fair degree of accuracy what the size of the population in a
given region of the globe will be in the year 2,000
and the probable extent of urbanization; we have some
idea where scholarship is leading, and—at least for a
decade at a time—what advances are being made in our
scientific laboratories.

From present indications we can draw up a number
of postulates concerning what is termed the material
cause of the Church, which is mankind, to whom the
Church has been sent and of whom it is composed.
Admittedly these are external facts for the most part
and are indicative only to a limited extent. Even more
actual enlightenment comes from an awareness of
present-day movements and the directions they are
taking, especially those having a vital dynamism. This
includes modern currents in the world of ideas and
ventures deliberately undertaken for which we can pre-
dict the outcome and impact, either in the near future
or even at a more remote time, for example, two generations from now. We can anticipate the life of the
man of tomorrow on the basis of what we see around
us today: on the one hand, certain needs; and on the
other certain forces, actual or potential.

There remain, however, some unknown factors that qualify our expectations. We must consider the incredible complexity of prevailing conditions, the vast sphere of the unforeseeable, the play of wills, and finally the fulfillment of time as it pertains to the Church. For the Church has its own particular time, which complicates every prediction of her future. The future of the Church depends on the Holy Spirit and on prayer. (It is a little bit understandable why an American sociologist, Louis Wirth, wrote: "If you would be a sociologist, the first thing to do is throw all notion of the supernatural out the window.") Time for the Church is not simply the period of temporal history through which she must pass and on which she must register an impression. Even now human history is not simply a record of time charted by the movements of the stars; rather we count in years; and while the years may be measured by the revolutions of the earth around the sun, we also mark them off by reigns and governments, cataclysms, wars, revolutions, great inventions, and works of genius.

The history of the Church is part of this history of mankind, but it has its own rhythm, scored by initiatives that spring not only from the freedom of men but also from the freedom of the godhead, which is to say, divine grace. The whole subject of conversion comes into it. And from a spiritual point of view, history is governed by and organized around occasions of conversion. There is not only the conversion from unbelief to faith of those who hear the Word and accept it, there is also the perpetual process of conversion going on even in those who should be bearers of the Word and who, first of all and for that very reason, must foster its growth in themselves. Therefore, in addition to what we might call historic changes of heart that have social or literary repercussions, there are those intimate conversions of each one of us that transform us and are communicated to others who, in their turn, become agents or occasions for change, in a way that is as unlimited as it is unpredictable. The whole Church is both a place and a means of conversion to the Gospel.

Conversion always means an internal change in the Church; but there are also conversions that have a more social impact. Their effects are felt not only in the Communion of Saints, but also in the structures and activities of the visible society of the Church. When such an occurrence is widespread or has a radically renewing effect, we call it a reform. The Church must be and actually is constantly reforming herself because, although truly the Body of Christ, nonetheless it never measures up to its Head, her sovereign Prince and principle, Jesus Christ. He is the perfect fulfillment of the reign and grace of God. He is in his body as the life of that body, but in such a way that he remains transcendent, as its arbiter, its standard, and its Lord. Thus St. Paul wrote that the body must grow up in him who is the Head, *eis auton hos estin è kephalè, Christos*

(Eph. 4:15), from whom it receives congruity and coherence. Hence it derives its increase from the building up of itself in love.

Reforms are a conforming to Christ, new attempts to adapt to the Gospel. Those same adjustments, in response to the same kind of necessity, are also adaptations to history aimed at bringing about the encounter of Christ and the world and interpreting the content of the Scriptures *for* the world at a given point in its history. Reforms, therefore, have two ends: they are a response to two vocations or summonses, that of Christ and the Gospel to be developed *in us*; and that of Christ and the Gospel to be given *to the world*. The primary thing in either case is the demands of the Gospel, and then their application to the circumstances of our own lives and to the needs of the world and the times. Indeed, the Church has its own growth and development which must be in conformity with Christ, its Lord, but it exists *for mankind* whom it must strive to transform into the People of God, the Body of Christ, and the Temple of the Holy Spirit. Thus the demands for renewal and reform come to the Church from two directions. She has repeatedly had to revise forms that became inadequate, so that Life in the larger sense would not be undermined by life in the narrow sense, shriveled to the scale of habit and convenience. The really great moments in the past history of the Church are those in which it has undertaken just such renovations; the great moments in its future, which is only history still unwritten, will be no different. But our timidity and lack of imagination and initiative are astounding.

On the basis of the criteria and limitations just mentioned, I am going to try to sketch a rough outline of what I see as the tendencies that will affect the future of the Church. I do so still under the influence of my experience at the Second Vatican Council, mindful as much of texts considered there as of a host of vital, refreshing contacts with men from all over the world. What I am going to say, I am well aware, is partly wishful, but is not mere dreaming. Perhaps it will seem terribly idealistic, but I am the first to concede that my own mediocrity disqualifies me from doing any programming. Nevertheless I am convinced that this outline is drawn from viable traits efficacious for the future, actual tendencies already at work, seeds already planted and even now beginning to burst their coats and send up shoots.

I have elsewhere used this formula several times: a Church that is less *of* the world and more *to* the world. The same formula will help organize what I have to say here. It expresses precisely the change that is, in fact, taking place—or trying to—and there are signs of it. Let us examine how it may come to be.

We have referred to a Church that is less *of the World*. First of all, it is less part of a *specific* world in which for centuries it has had a precarious foothold where it stamped its character. The foothold is precarious, because any hold is only temporary; although this has been a relatively long-lasting one, fairly satisfactory, passably represented in the social institutions. We refer to that state of Christendom that is conveniently called Constantinian, but is more especially medieval. It is characterized by the fact that the monarchs, that is, the Church's counterpart of authority in the sphere of government, are so integrated into the Church that they are like her ministers for external affairs, the temporal and the spiritual being fused into a single body politic, governed in principle by the hierarchy. The Church ("Holy Church," as she began to be called after the end of the thirteenth century, referring to the juridical person, subject of rights, privileges, and powers) obviously found this to her advantage: she could govern the conduct of men in accordance with her ends and her laws. For a long time she enjoyed a monopoly on the manifestations of culture, beauty, and opinion. Even those who rebelled against her exercise of authority claimed to have no other Mother and to seek no hearth but hers.

In this symbiotic relationship with the secular powers, the Church unfortunately took on the air and trappings of aristocracy, with the result that, under the feudal institutions and mentality in which she lived for so long, it came to seem necessary for authority to be identified with titles of rank and property. Even theology found in Scholasticism a form so perfectly fitting that in our day we tend to equate one with the other. Yet the Middle Ages were strictly Western and Latin. Although certainly the Greek Fathers were not unknown, adequate lines of communication with the Eastern tradition were not maintained and sight was lost of the fact that the East had a complete and coherent heritage, with a weight and validity similar to those of the Latin tradition. A complete world, enclosed, homogeneous, sure of herself, Medieval Christendom hardly knew what dialogue meant. Who was there to engage in it with her? It was as if she held a sleeping world cradled in her arms: *tanquam sopita civitate mundi,* wrote Otto Von Freising in the middle of the twelfth century. And when the world awoke, when it began to loosen the clasp and go its own way, the Church for a long time did not quite take the change seriously. She tried to go on holding society by the hand, correcting it, making it recite its lessons. But it was already too big, too strong, and too far away.

Taking a step forward out of the Middle Ages does not mean displacing the Faith from its primal position or depreciating the splendid synthesis Scholasticism achieved. It does mean acknowledging the existence of the world and scrutinizing ourselves for vestiges of worldly and aristocratic pretensions. The future of the Church lies in this direction. The first step, namely, full recognition of the reality of the world around us, is entirely consonant with the Church's increasing awareness that she is not the same as the world, that she may be only the Church, but that she *is* that!

Of course, the Church cannot bypass the temporal order. Indeed it has too many ties with secular society not to try to organize or regulate it in the interests of both parties as well as for the sake of harmony. Certainly, too, the Church has a hierarchical structure of which, naturally, there are visible signs. But these aspects of her existence must be utterly evangelical, purified of every presumption to a temporal kind of authority.

In the past ten years, I have been struck by what I call the recurrence of the Christian. This requires explanation, for there have always been true Christians. Before our times there were men who made efforts to refashion, in the spirit of the Gospel, the whole of their persons, and even their political and social action. But it seems that they were either exceptional personalities or men who represented the long arm of the Church, so to speak, in secular institutions. What is so impressive today is the number of men and women, oftentimes married couples, who, although they are entirely in the world, indistinguishable from the rest of the populace in their real, temporal involvements, are striving to be genuinely Christian to the very core of their mundane human existence and to live their Christian commitment with evangelical loyalty.

What is entirely new in this has, as I see it, two aspects. In the first place, instead of men who are fairly pagan and worldly-minded in their daily lives, but who bow to the laws of the Church, we have people aiming for Christian conduct in even the most ordinary facets of their temporal lives. In the second place, these persons are living their Christianity as a response to the demands of the world and life in it, but are governed by the spirit of the Gospel. Life for them is an apostolic responsibility for everything around them. They experience the demands of Christianity less as a set of regulations handed down once and for all by the Church—but external to their own consciences—than as a confrontation which life, events, and circumstances present to them as needs or opportunities for the light of the Gospel. This reformed way of life which has been called (perhaps uniquely in man's spiritual odyssey) an original initiative of the laity, arising as it did outside of monasteries and the ecclesiastical sphere, is a manifestation of what I am trying to describe. It is noteworthy that, typically, there are even communal efforts in this direction. Such instances, organized or individual, are both the effect and the sign of the re-emergence in our time of the true Christian.

A world that is fully "world," to the extent that it offers contradiction and challenge, gives rise to such Christians. Of course, it results in a tremendous falling away of the masses of folk who submit or are subject to social pressures. Thus it has become one of the tasks of Catholic Action groups to alter or channel those pressures toward a more favorable outcome. But the end of the Constantinian era, the fact that today there is no longer such a thing as a self-contained world, at least none freely self-contained, means that we have entered upon a religiously pluralist world society in which real Christians, the faithful, will be only a fraction of the whole, often a minority. Father Karl Rahner has quite justifiably written of a situation of *diaspora*.

Thus the future of the Church falls to a minority who are conscious of having ultimate responsibility for all and of having a mission to all of mankind. A small Church in a vast world, but a fledgling Church, a leavening Church, and a Church-sacrament-sign of universal salvation! This situation makes enormous demands. The challenge which the reaction of the world makes to our faith forces us to be genuinely what we profess to be. Such a challenge calls for a deeper personal assimilation and integration of our convictions and conduct. As a corollary, it impels the clergy to make even greater efforts toward formation in the faith and personal prayer, and thus to see themselves as less confined to the service of the altar, or rather, to look upon the ministrations of worship, for which they have the responsibility, as a service to faith, not as mere service of "a religion." "Religion" pays its dues to God, but faith devotes its whole life to his reign. Religion is a separate order of activities; faith transforms every activity and calls nothing profane except what sin profanes by removing it from the offering of all things to God.

If the future of the Church tends in this direction, the future of ecclesiology will correspond, for there is a congruity between them. Today, wherever we find a pre-Constantinian situation, it is no coincidence that we find the kind of theological thinking and approach to problems that was typical of the early Fathers. In emerging from the Middle Ages and the Counter Reformation, we are abandoning the juridicism that has pervaded the very modes of thought from the end of the thirteenth century onwards.

The conscience of the Church as it spoke through the Vatican Council in October of 1963 gives precedence to the ontology of grace over institutions of ecclesiastical law and office, which are not thereby repudiated but only relegated to their proper place in the service of an order of being (grace), a supernatural reality having a sacramental basis. The Church becomes once again the People of God made up of Christians, and not merely a juridical entity, a moral person, possessor of rights, able, if necessary, to exist by itself without the whole Christian people. We rediscover this notion in the writings of the Fathers, in the liturgy, and, of course, in the New Testament only by a serious study of the texts. I believe it cannot better be described than by calling it an ecclesiology which encompasses a Christian anthropology, or else by a term I referred to before, ontology of grace, an order of being manifested by a Church made up of Christians, the baptized, who offer their lives and actions as a spiritual sacrifice and live in the spirit of the Gospel. The future of the Church will be that of a People of God who are conscious of this identity, ever alert to changing events in order to take on their Christian responsibility in the world. They will be a priesthood served by ordained members who are responsible for ministering the Faith through them and promoting the development of the Christian person.

This presumes a declericalization of the idea of the Church, too often seen as a block of liturgical "practitioners" with the laity as clientele. It was a Church seen in its own institutional structure, considered to be of absolute and primal importance, instead of having importance in reference to the Christian person. The new attitude calls for an end to the juridicism that has pervaded the Catholic body to an incredible degree: sacraments and liturgy, prayer and morality, intramural contacts, etc.

These are some of the major items on the agenda for a Church which is to be less *of* the world, and which may be only the Church, but will *be* that!

A Church oriented *to* the world will, by reason of that fact, first of all realistically acknowledge the world that confronts her. A Church whose whole existence, even those elements in it that exist simply to praise God, which I would not overlook, has, like a dimension enhancing all that she is, the conviction and pervasive awareness of having been *sent* to that world. The future of the Church is, in this sense, entirely missionary. And it will be a future of dialogue. The two, mission and dialogue, are not inimical to one another except superficially. That is what I will try to demonstrate here, aware as I am that this is the very life-blood of her continued existence.

Within the stronghold of Christendom, the Church really had no world to face. She had, for all practical purposes, assimilated and formed it in her image, with the result that there was scarcely any tension or dialogue except with her own kind. Now, dialogue, like mission, always supposes another recognized as other, yet capable of communion. In our time the Church can hardly fail to be aware of a dynamic, investigating, inquisitive world. And this world is challenging her, sometimes by a sharp and violent confrontation, sometimes by its utter indifference, which is the same as charging her with being empty and irrelevant. Hence the Church, conscious of her mission to the world, must seek a real encounter. No longer enjoying a monopoly as she did in times past, she must first of all engage the attention of mankind, and to do so she has to take the initiative by interesting herself in the concerns of people. It is no longer acceptable for her simply to cast her Message before the world without inquiring first what the world is, what its potentialities are, and what it has of value. For the past twenty years now, serious reflection on the internal mission of the Church has led to an understanding of it not as a unilateral giving but as including a responsibility to acquire a certain receptivity, a welcoming openness to others, a willingness for exchange, for reciprocity, and ultimately for sharing.

In listening to and meeting missionaries and bishops

from developing Christian outposts assembled at the Vatican Council, we have been struck by their concurrence on two basic points. First, they no longer want to hear of "the missions," but rather of *the mission* of the Church, for the whole Church has a mandate and is missionary in all that she does. Secondly, they stress the need for taking into account (after cautious evaluation of what is involved) the fact that, in all men, in all peoples, and even in religions objectively false, there are sparks of grace and truth that come from the Word and that enlighten us all; tidings which we have, incarnate, in the Suffering Servant of all mankind whose name is Jesus Christ. Obviously this viewpoint will have to support the missionary approach and the theological research connected with it during forthcoming decades. It coincides rather remarkably with the studies that can be made (I myself have made such a study) concerning the coming to the Faith as revealed in the Scriptures, especially in St. John's Gospel with its theology of signs. It thus becomes apparent that dialogue is not simply a matter of intellectual contacts specifically conducted on the level of ecumenism. Rather, the mission and, we may say, *grace itself*, have a dialogical cast. In this mission, the fullness of truth, who is Christ, encounters and takes up into himself all seeds of truth; and absolute Grace, who is Christ, encounters rudimentary deposits of grace and sometimes an inchoate Christianity, lacking, for the most part, baptism and the name of Christian. Missionary and, to some extent, even pastoral theology—if indeed they are different from one another—in the future ought to give a large place to all that is implicitly Christian and its relation to what is explicitly Christian, avoiding syncretism, mere convenience, rash zeal, and all such pitfalls.

A Church that is oriented increasingly *to* the world, we said. What world? A world bursting with inquiries and inventions, but also a world wracked with suffering and which, because of the ease and frequency of individual contacts, so readily achieved with our media of information and communication, has taken on an entirely unprecedented, acute, and even explosive awareness of the current world-wide phenomena of hunger and underdevelopment. Of course it is not up to the Church to find technical solutions for the problems of the hungry and underdeveloped nations, nor even for the problem of world peace, but, in the name of the Gospel that has been entrusted to her, the Church, as God's People, ought to bring about some changes in the situation. Even in the Old Testament, the covenant with God required that certain demands in justice be met, as we see, for example, in the Book of Amos. Moreover, Messianic salvation and peace are not simply ultimate or eschatological, for the end of time has already begun, the kingdom is working itself out. Therefore, the mission of Christ was foretold by the prophets and proclaimed by Jesus himself as a command "to seek and to save what was lost" (Luke 19:10), . . . "to proclaim to the captives release and sight to the blind, to set at liberty the oppressed . . ." (Luke 4:19). Granted, then:

The Church is not responsible for bringing technical solutions to the problems of hunger and economic development. But there are three things she should do. She ought to step down and live with the poor. Not that it isn't already being done, for in some instances she is deeply submerged in poverty, but a tremendous effort remains to be made along these lines. This was a subject for thought and work among several different groups of bishops at the Council. And she ought to spend herself to the utmost—as if it were a matter of keen urgency—to find means of establishing a true spirit of community. We know that one of the first and essential messages of the Gospel is the injunction to all men to love one another and to share with one another. Along with this goes a duty to denounce all inhuman and anti-Christian economic structures existing solely for profit and having no regard for men and their betterment. She should also elicit and accept the necessary mediations and initiatives of the laity, without which the step from message to effective action will hardly be taken, even by a People of God whose highly-developed notions of the protocols of priority and authority have given way before a universal awareness of the needs of the times and a common dedication to the Church's mission. There seems to be no doubt that all this will be of major importance in the future of the Church. Moreover, this future of mission and dialogue will include the uplifting of the world's down-trodden and, quite literally, a crusade, a wholly peaceful one, of sharing and giving.

The world to which the Church has been sent is not only a deprived world but a divided one as well. This also weighs heavily on consciences in modern times. From a Christian viewpoint, it is a world throbbing with ecumenical aspirations and endeavors. This brings us to one of the key questions in the future of the Catholic Church, namely, to what extent will Catholicism be open to ecumenical exploration? That is to say, how far can it go in surmounting the consciousness of being adequately the Church in order to concede that the Church transcends all ecclesiastical institutions and exists to some degree or other in all Christian communions? That question was raised recently by the Reverend Marc Boegner, writing in *Le Figaro,* as well as by numerous observers at the Council, among them Professor Edmund Schlink in a talk he gave on October 23, 1963.

This delicate question gives rise to another, not very familiar in our theology, concerning the role of the Holy Spirit, that is, the ever-present reality of divine action in relation to existing structures, even authentic and sacred ones. To cite another unknown: what, ultimately, will ecumenism bring to the Catholic Church? It has already meant a great deal, that much is certain, for at least indirectly and sometimes directly the Orthodox and Protestants have been our benefactors. To what extent will contact with them, the fact that there is contact, lead us—and them—to develop unitive attitudes? The future of the Church, her conception of herself and her conception of her hierarchy, ministry, and sacraments depends in a large measure on that, but the outcome remains problematical.

Finally, what means will ecumenism use? Surely it will continue the ones it has been using up to now: information, dialogue, a return to the sources, joint prayer. Other ways, although comparatively unprecedented, are not inconceivable: for example, increased collective action, not only on the level of social action consonant with the Natural Law and the Decalogue, but specifically on the level of Christian labor in the vineyard. Consider, for example, the East, where the two Churches have fundamentally the same dogmatic and sacramental substance: should Catholics, making no stipulations except respect for their loyalty to Catholicism, put themselves at the service of the Orthodox Churches? Would that be impossible? Not at all, because it is already being done. In Rome recently a Catholic priest, vowed to a life among the poor, mentioned to a Protestant observer his ambition to see the Church break out of her shell, so to speak, away from her family and her own kind, and walk among the poor of the world, preaching the Gospel and bringing them freedom. The priest asked the observer for his reaction to the idea, and the reply was: "That would be a real Reformation! In the sixteenth century the Reformers wanted to remake the Church; they failed and went on to found their own Church. But if, now, together, we were to reach out to the poor . . . !"

Such speculation may sound like romantic fantasizing, but I would like to point out one thing: over and over again it happened at the Council that a text drawn up the previous day, or the day before that, already seemed dated. This happened with the Schema on the Pastoral Office of Bishops, on which discussion continues; in the light of the Schema on the Church and the vote of October 30, 1963, by which the Assembly declared its considered opinion, the former, when presented, looked more like a piece from the days of Pius IX or Pius XII than of John XXIII and Paul VI. This was even true of a text like the draft decree on Ecumenism. After the addresses of the Holy Father, given as early as September and October of 1962, the draft lacked something: today it could go much further. Things are moving quickly now.

Dreams and visions? Let me add that we do not know what may happen in this field that is so newly apparent as certain to play a role in the future of the Church. It is significant to observe how the different topics we have touched upon affect one another: World; Dialogue and Mission; Mission and Sharing; Ecumenism and the steps toward a point of convergence. These are all contributing forces in a basically single thrust forward, a leap from an institutionally self-centered state to one oriented *toward mankind*. Professor K. E. Skydsgaard referred to this in an address to the Holy

Father, delivered in behalf of the observer-delegates to the Council, on October 17, 1963.

We have an active world, already burgeoning with fruitful notions, but at the same time suffering from privations and dissensions. Let us now add for completion: we have a world straining for unification but isolating itself into separate sectors and local entities, sometimes out of national solidarity, sometimes on a continental scale. And the processes are going on simultaneously. Just when this planet has every reason to achieve unity, various social and cultural segments of it are coming separately alive to unify local domestic problems, needs, and resources.

The Church is beginning to adjust to this relatively new situation. Will it shock you if I say that the Church, indisputably Catholic in the dogmatic sense of that word, is not really catholic in structure? I grasped that fact a bit better when I considered both what actual chance there is, for instance, for the Eastern Tradition in the Catholic Church, and the example of the World Council of Churches in Geneva, which holds its assemblies equally well in Buenos Aires or Ceylon or Singapore, Lund or Toronto. *Our* modern Ecumenical Council convenes in Rome. Moreover, from a practical viewpoint, it is fairly difficult to imagine that it could be held anywhere else, although nothing keeps us from realizing that the outcome of a good many issues would certainly be different if it were held, say, in New Delhi or in Dakar.

The Church is catholic, but she is organized along centralist, imperialist lines. And there is no denying the fact that Catholicism is not strongly represented on a world scale. Asia nurtures (although how inadequately!) more than fifty per cent of the world population, five per cent of which is Christian, two and one-half per cent being Catholic. What, specifically, has she brought to the Council? to the life of the Church? Whatever the answer, there is no reason for pessimism because progress can be so swift. In 1959 Pope John requested reports from bishops all over the world detailing matters they felt the Council should take up. I thought, after reading the suggestions, that Africa and even South America would have very little to contribute to the Council. But I was wrong. Those two continents gave evidence of dynamic force.

In any case, revision of the internal structure of the Church to make it clearly more global in scope has already begun at the Council, and a certain amount of authority, still to be defined, has been ceded to national conferences of bishops on the basis of the principle of episcopal collegiality. Along with this step goes the promise, or at least intimation of the intentions of the Holy Father, to bring about a reform of the Curia. The very word *collegiality* seems to have become almost a good omen. Time will put an end to dreaming, but that doctrine, now definitely enunciated, is tremendously significant. According to the definition, supreme authority in the Church is not solely monarchical, it is *both* monarchical, or primatial, *and* collegial by divine right. Thus, when the Holy Father wishes (and even in his inaugural address he implied it was possible) to include residential bishops in the central governing body of the Church, conceivably even attaching a sort of permanent synod representative of all the Churches to decide major questions, he will be acting on a doctrinal basis laid down by the Council. The doctrine also recognizes that the bishops form a body of which they become a part by reason of their episcopal consecration. By that anointing, in communion with the whole body and its head, the pope, they are given the duty and the necessary powers to preach the Gospel, administer the sacraments, and shepherd the Church of God. And for each one this responsibility is universal, to be exercised corporately with all other bishops, recognizing that, for good order and concord, each has actual power of government over a specific portion of the flock. In other words, the bishop's office carries at one and the same time a world-wide responsibility shared in mutual solidarity by all bishops, and a geographically delimited governing power.

These principles are to be interpreted on the practical plane by local, national, and continental conferences and through a reciprocating system of lateral lines of communication and relationships extending horizontally, so to speak, instead of converging, as before, on one central peak, the apex of a pyramid. It is probable that Vatican Council II has reopened the chapter on what may be called the conciliar or synodal life of the Church. I refer, of course, to the various assemblies just named, whether centralized or particular to the separate segments of the one body which is made up not only of persons but of peoples. In the sphere of ecclesiology, all this calls for a theology of the whole Church seen as a Communion of local Churches, a rich theology which, since it parallels the conception of authority as a service and a responsibility, could inspire reform in the practical exercise of that power. Here too, rigid juridicism now gives way before the establishment of more interior ties and relationships, which may take on a spiritual tenor, since they more directly invoke the Christian person which every member of the hierarchy remains. Often quoted in recent times as offering a solution to so many difficulties are these words of St. Augustine: "Vobis sum episcopus, vobiscum christianus" ("For you I am a bishop, but with you I am a Christian").

I have no doubt that these changes will come within the purview of the Church of the future or that they fall within the realm of reasonable probability.

I would like now to add a few final thoughts. The future of the Church is in and to the world, and, in more than one respect, is bound to the future of the human race, but there is a pivotal factor that lies at the very center of the Church itself. The innovations we have outlined call for a certain kind of Christian and a certain kind of priest. We can anticipate this as much from clear indications visible today as from tomorrow's needs or past and present examples. To cite one current example: having several times felt a good deal of respect for the admirable intellectual outlook of some of the Latin American bishops, I began (because my reaction, which does me no credit, was one of surprise) to look for an explanation of it.

I learned that it rose originally from a single Faculty of Theology, that of Santiago de Chile, and then from a few others, Buenos Aires, for example. This fact is a vindication of the old position of the Order of Preachers, of Gerson, and of the Christian humanists at Louvain and Paris, who advocated education. Given a high level of theological teaching entirely open to university-type research and not simply dedicated to the ritual transmission of stock knowledge, a good many possibilities open up. This is essential if we are to carry on the enormous task of moving into the world and engaging in dialogue with that world-in-fermentation. There is no need to know everything and even less to pretend that we do. How much appreciated, for example, was the attitude of His Holiness, Pope Paul VI, in speaking to members of the Congress of Space Medicine. He said to them: "You know more than I about this, so you must do the talking. . . . But there is a point in your investigations where dialogue is possible and on which I will have something to say: the subject is man, who is our common concern."

Let us go even beyond the subject of man to the very heart of reality, concerning which there is some-

thing that should be said here. During the past ten
years or more, a conviction has been taking shape in
my mind, arising partly from my reflections on the
problems raised by Christian life in a secular world
and partly from a disinterested study of Holy Scriptures. The conviction is this: Nothing decisive will
be accomplished until we return to a genuinely biblical
idea of God as the *Living* God, proposed to our *Faith*.
I said *Living* God; he is not simply a God unto himself, having no connection with creation, but a God
who calls on us freely to co-operate with him by re-
laying his action in the world and to other men. And
I use the words, *proposed to our Faith*: he is not a
God who is simply the recipient of our homage, in
line with the vertical orientation of "Religion." Rather,
he is a God active in us, a God who carries out in
the world and in us a design or a plan in which we
are invited to incorporate ourselves by opening up to
him in faith the "unlimited credit" on which he counts
to bring about his reign and be truly God in our lives.

In this perspective, *everything* that man accomplishes
in Faith and because of Faith, out of obedience to God
and the will to be simply and totally what he wishes,
everything, I say, is matter for the spiritual offering we
are invited to make. In making that offering, everyone is his own priest, although its consummation should
be with the community of the faithful in union with
Christ's perfect sacrifice which the priest offers sacra-
mentally on the altar. There is a narrowing of the

gap between what is done in the Church as an order apart, and what is done in the world. The Church will be seen to have fully inserted herself in the world in the midst of which and for which she stands as the sacrament of its salvation, that is, of its fulfillment in God. Lay people are no longer to be looked upon as mere "clients" of the clergy nor defined in a clerical frame of reference. Every individual will be seen as a spark of light in the world, existing to be restored to God in Christ.

If the future of the Church is as I describe, this view must prevail. It requires an end to the disastrous separation too often made between what we call the Sacred and the Profane, the order of Redemption and the order of Creation. I am convinced that the affirmation of the Living God revealed in the Old Testament on the one hand and the true, scriptural notion of the liturgy and of sacrifice on the other provide all we need to enter into a very simple but very strong unity, interacting on the very loom of temporal life and world history, but still for the ends of Faith.

The future of the Church will depend to a large extent on the diffusion of this message, without timidity or regret for a past of ceremonial and clerical ritual. There are many other things to say on this subject, but, like St. John, I content myself with pointing out that, "If every one of them should be written, not even the world itself, I think, could hold the books that would have to be written." Let it be enough that perspectives have been opened up. The future, by definition, is an opening, not a closing. Nor is it entirely undesirable that a paper on the future of the Church should come to an end without a conclusion. We have just crossed a threshold.